WHO'S IN CHARGE?

Also by Philip Seib

The Art of Politics with James Brown
Dallas: Chasing the Urban Dream
Getting Elected

WHO'S IN CHARGE?

HOW THE MEDIA SHAPE NEWS AND POLITICIANS WIN VOTES

PHILIP SEIB

TAYLOR PUBLISHING COMPANY
DALLAS, TEXAS

Published by Taylor Publishing Company
1550 West Mockingbird Lane
Dallas, Texas 75235

Library of Congress Cataloging-in-Publication Data

Seib, Philip M., 1949–
    Who's in charge : how the media shape news and politicians
win votes / Philip Seib.
        p.   cm.
    Bibliography: p.
    Includes index.
    ISBN 0–87833–583–8 : $14.95
    1. Electioneering—United States.   2. Voting—United States.
3. Mass media—Political aspects—United States.   I. Title.
JK2281.S46 1988
324′.4—dc19   87-28810
                                                            CIP

ISBN: 0–87833–583–8

Printed in the United States of America

10 9 8 7 6 5 4 3 2 1

Contents

Preface

The spring of 1987 was warmed by two political bonfires. One had been carefully constructed with plenty of kindling and aged wood, nurtured for months as the first wisps of smoke led to flickering sparks and then roaring flames. The other appeared with such blazing suddenness that it seemed a case of spontaneous combustion.

The Iran-contra scandal and the precipitous demise of Gary Hart had much in common. They both involved personal and political intrigue. They offered examples of monumental lapses of judgment by leaders who had been expected to behave better. They provided enough gossip to keep political junkies happy for months. And they both owed much of their incendiary visibility to the news media.

Yet the arms-for-hostages scheme was slowly unearthed by the efforts of persistent reporters and government investigators. The reportage took time to develop and was met with great resistance from those who preferred the even ground of the status quo rather than a field plowed by inquiry.

Hart's soap opera, on the other hand, lasted only a week, from the initial revelations of his alleged fling with a young woman to his withdrawal from the presidential race.

Singly and together, these cases provide insight into the power wielded by the news media. Journalists didn't create these issues; reporters didn't sell arms or procure women. But members of the press nevertheless made certain the public was aware of these dramas, and they kept attention focused on the politicians until some resolution of the matters at hand was reached.

The ramifications were substantial. A popular president, re-elected just three years earlier in a massive landslide, suddenly found his previously adoring public didn't trust him. An ambitious young politician, well on his way to his party's presidential nomination and perhaps on to the White House, suddenly found his career in ruins.

Did the news media "get" these two men? No, they got themselves. Despite these politicians' assertions that they had been mistreated in news coverage, the press merely pointed the spotlight and made certain it kept shining.

Such events have happened before and they'll happen again. In some form or another, news reaches virtually everyone who isn't living in a cave. This pervasiveness ensures a continuing tension between media and politics. Media professionals and politicians enjoy a not-so-peaceful coexistence; they know they need each other, but that doesn't mean they have to like each other.

Too often you, the voter and news consumer, may feel like an outsider as these powerful forces pursue their joint and separate interests. This book is for you, to help you examine the relationship between press and politicians and understand how other media forces—such as campaign advertising—shape our political world.

By looking at recent political history, I've found examples of how news people and politicians do their jobs—what their motivations and standards are, how they work with and against each other, and how they feel about you, the individual who frequently becomes lost in that amorphous mass known as "the public."

I've spent a number of years on both sides of the political fence, first as a pol, advising and managing campaigns, and later as a print and television journalist, covering the politicians. Such experience produces sagacity or schizophrenia or, most likely, a little of both. That history, plus my frequent dissatisfaction with the content of campaigns and of their coverage, provided the impetus for writing this book.

1 | Politicians and the News Media

When Dan Rather introduces a CBS story about President Reagan by saying, "It was another day filled with photo opportunities," how do you react? Do you follow Rather's lead and watch Reagan with the scorn appropriate for a manipulative politician? Or do you resent Rather's implicit editorializing and watch the President sympathetically, seeing him as the victim of Rather's bias?

"Pure" journalism (if such exists) would present Reagan without creating viewer predispositions one way or the other. A neutral introduction such as, "President Reagan made these public appearances today . . ." would let viewers decide for themselves how political or presidential Reagan was.

Journalists might argue that neutrality actually works in the politician's favor. A skilled campaigner, such as an incumbent president, can stage events he claims are part of his official duties, when they are really nothing more than thinly disguised vote-seeking. The voter, the journalist might say, needs to be told about this artifice so he will not be conned by the politician.

This argument is well taken, but it is based on two debatable premises: First, that the politician is acting with nefarious ulterior motives; and second, that the news consumer is too slow-witted to figure things out for himself.

1

This instance and others like it beg the larger question of how much responsibility the press should take in leading public opinion. This question pervades most of the issues in the press-politics relationship. No satisfactory answer has been found.

From college classrooms to cocktail parties, candidates and anchormen provide fuel for substantive debate and titillating gossip. Politics is a spectator sport for most people. Actual participation is infrequent, limited to an occasional trip to a polling place to vote. Only a minuscule part of the electorate gets more involved, such as by doing volunteer work for a candidate.

But the voter is also a news consumer. Even if he does nothing more than cast a ballot once every four years in a presidential race, the voter is often the recipient of a flood of political information delivered by the news media. And unless he makes a determined effort to shut off the flow of news, his attitudes about politics are being shaped—subtly but constantly—by this information.

Voting behavior is something like a psychological jigsaw puzzle: Many tiny pieces, none of which might be of much significance by itself, finally take the form of an understandable picture. Often this picture doesn't take its ultimate shape until a few days or even a few hours before voting begins, but it is this "picture" that is carried into the voting booth when an individual casts a ballot.

Pieces of this puzzle come from diverse sources. Some are supplied directly by politicians via direct-mail brochures, billboard messages, or television ads. Some pieces come from friends, family members, or other sources that, no matter how far removed they are from politics, still influence our thinking about politics.

For example, if a man works in a factory and belongs to a union, he might think of the union principally as his champion in matters of wages and working conditions. But before election day, he's likely to hear that the union is backing a particular candidate. Its predisposition will affect his own. Or if in casual conversation his next-door neighbor offers a few words of praise or condemnation of an office seeker, or at church his minister makes comments in support of a particular issue, these voices cannot help but contribute to this man's eventual voting decision.

Probably, however, the most consistent suppliers of political information to all voters are newspapers, television, and radio. Politics is big business not just for the candidates, but also for the news organizations that cover government and the electoral process. Rare is the campaign that doesn't rely on "media events" to display its wares to the voters. Equally rare is the news organization that doesn't spend much time and money trying to make political coverage palatable to an audience that is only mildly interested in politics.

This relationship, however, is flawed. Despite the importance of the press as the principal conveyor of political information to the electorate, too few reporters know all they should about the issues and campaign techniques they cover. Similarly, few politicians understand the complexities and responsibilities of the news business.

Conflicts between politician and reporter (such as the occasional dueling between Ronald Reagan and ABC's Sam Donaldson) are unavoidable, but how disruptive such friction is can be determined to a considerable extent by the degree of understanding each side possesses about the other.

Any reporter who covers campaigns should understand and respect (one requires the other) the professional and personal components of a politician's life:

• Most politicians are keenly ambitious and realize how intensely competitive their profession is. What motivates the pol to undergo the rigors of campaigning? What does the candidate hope to accomplish in terms of issues and his career?

• Politics has been described as the art of compromise, but compromise cannot exist without some boundaries. Are contributions and endorsements contingent on the candidate's taking prescribed positions? What happens when such pressures conflict with conscience?

• Political technologies in matters such as polling and voter contact are evolving rapidly. Given the nature of the race, are appropriately sophisticated and tested techniques being used to implement the campaign's strategy? How have the strategies worked in previous campaigns?

• Politics operates according to complex sets of rules that must be well understood by all serious candidates. What are the guidelines governing voting procedures, election laws, and the rest of the mechanical framework within which a campaign must operate?

Similarly, politicians should know and respect how the news media work:

- The journalist doesn't operate in a vacuum. What does the press expect from the politician? What do reporters need—such as advance schedules, filing time, and regular access to the candidate—in order to do their jobs?
- Journalists work under technical constraints that can affect how they do their job. What limitations such as deadlines and electronic transmission logistics affect the scope of news coverage?
- Like politicians, journalists are ambitious men and women who understand the competitiveness of their profession. What motivates the political reporter? How might covering a campaign help or hinder a reporter's career, and how does it affect his or her personal life?
- Journalism is a business, and reporters are often reminded of the importance of their news organization's bottom line. What commercial demands are part of the reporter's approach to political coverage? How do circulation figures and rating points help decide what is covered?

Compounding the difficulties inherent in the press-politician relationship is the public's limited understanding of how either side operates.

Such difficulties are exacerbated by nonchalant attitudes about political news coverage. When viewers become too comfortable, accepting a campaign as being merely a series of media events and evaluating a political report as if it was merely a rerun of "Miami Vice," they limit their power to meaningfully affect election outcomes. Just as politics suffers because too many persons consider it foreign to their own experience, so too does news coverage suffer because its audience is too undemanding.

Although few people will ever be presidential candidates, we are all voters who need to maintain a certain level of political awareness in order to be able to cast a well-informed ballot. Similarly, few people will ever become network anchors, but we're all likely to be regular news consumers; we should be able to evaluate the quality of the information the news media provide.

Such evaluation must include an analysis of the whys and wherefores of public opinion. Public attitudes about most politicians, for instance, are rooted in suspicion. Perhaps this cynicism is unwarranted, but Watergate, the Iran-contra scandal, and many other lesser offenses have made people wary about politicians' motives and intentions. Yet politicians often blame the press for nurturing negative public opinion. The pols claim that reporters too often try to be fashionably nasty, concentrating on finding public officials' failings and ignoring "good news." Thus the public receives a steady diet of negative coverage (or so this argument goes) that increases distrust.

Survey research generally indicates that voters do trust journalists more than politicians. This faith, however, is far from absolute. For example, in libel cases during the past few years, juries have assessed massive damages against news organizations. And in 1983, the public strongly supported the Reagan administration's exclusion of news media from the early stages of the invasion of Grenada. This wariness about the press is at least in part a logical reaction to the massive power the news media wield.

Just as one would expect a political candidate to have a hidden agenda of personal ambitions, one should have similar expectations regarding the press. The battle for ratings, the influence of editorial judgments and biases, and the personal ambitions of journalists have all attracted more attention as journalists (particularly television reporters and anchors) have become celebrities. A single rating point on a network's evening newscast can be worth more than $10 million in advertising revenue in a year. You—the newscast viewer and target of ratings competition—know this is a high-stakes game.

Suspicion about the press, as about any powerful institution, is fundamentally healthy. But if such suspicion reaches the point where the individual citizen trusts no one, the political system will deteriorate.

News audiences must also grapple with questions about *which* media sources they should rely on. A Gallup survey conducted in 1981 for *Newsweek* magazine found that Americans rated network television as the most reliable news source. When asked, "How good a job do different media do in providing accurate, unbiased news accounts?" respondents gave "Excellent/good" ratings in this order: network television, 71 percent; local television, 69 percent; news magazines, 66 percent; daily newspapers, 57 percent; personality/show business publications, 21 percent.

Each of these ratings except the last is evidence of substantial public faith in the news media. (This poll was taken soon after the

Janet Cooke scandal at the *Washington Post*. Newspaper reporters must have gnashed their teeth when they saw television news with a favorable rating so much greater than theirs.)

Heavy reliance on television has special significance in political coverage. In general terms, however, faith in television news reflects a relatively recent phenomenon that has occurred during the past three decades as the television set has become a standard item in virtually every American household.

Television news has weaknesses as well as strengths. The brevity of television newscasts demonstrates both of these. Because the news is available in concise, easily understandable form, more people avail themselves of this information. But too many of these people then think that they know all they need to know about complex subjects, when instead they have been exposed principally to headlines.

Walter Cronkite has said that he had wanted to end his newscasts by saying, "For more information, consult your local newspaper." But this extra effort of delving into print reports about the news items covered on television is beyond the ambition or ability of many people.

Television news also has a tendency to become hypnotized by its own technology. If a story about a less than crucial topic has attractive video or can incorporate snazzy graphics, and another more important story lacks pictures or is too complex to be "good television," many television news producers (particularly at local stations) will abandon the latter story.

Think how many times a local newscast features pictures from its "Eye in the Sky" helicopter even when the content of the story merits little or no coverage. If a station purchases an expensive toy, it will want to play with it. Granted, on many occasions the aerial newsgathering capability can enhance a report, but news value, not merely scintillating video, should dictate how scarce air time is allotted. The danger occurs when the tail is allowed to wag the dog.

This reaching for the lowest intellectual denominator is dictated, some television executives say, by the realities of broadcast economics. If the viewer can't understand a story, why put it on the air? Doing so will only lead the viewer to change channels and find a more palatable newscast; ratings of the high-minded channel will suffer. If this becomes conventional wisdom, the quality of television newscasts will sink into a bottomless pit.

Because of its pervasive influence, television news does much to set the intellectual level and tone of discourse about public issues. By setting high (but not unreachable) standards, television news can raise the level of this discourse, or it can lead the audience to believe that important issues are only matters of pretty pictures and simple choices.

If it resists such temptations, television news can capitalize on the inherent powers of the medium. The impact of its pictures cannot be overestimated. A classic example of this power is found in the coverage of the Vietnam War. For the first time, Americans in their living rooms were able to watch film footage of a war every evening. No longer was it just "war" as a remote political event; it became a savage, inescapable part of our daily lives.

Television coverage brought immediacy to the war, forcing us to think about just what was happening in Southeast Asia. Seeing those pictures every night made us ask questions, and from those questions evolved passions that shaped the politics of a decade.

The impact of television news is manifest in many ways. Sometimes it inspires debate about important issues. Sometimes it trivializes equally important matters. Sometimes it takes on the trappings of show business, making its reporters "stars" more than journalists.

The lead story on CBS or another network and the headline on the front page of *The New York Times* or other major newspaper are pronouncements by the news media that *these* are the important issues, these are what you should be paying attention to.

The news media may not tell us what to think, but they do tell us what to think about. This is power. Politicians recognize this, and realize that no politician—not even the president—will ever reach American public as frequently as does a network news anchorman. The opportunity a Dan Rather has to be heard by tens of millions of persons every weekday is the kind of access politicians can only dream about.

Setting the Agenda

By serving as the most constant provider of information to the public, the press does much to set the national agenda. The news media don't dictate ideology, but they do call their audiences' attention to certain issues. The story that merits a page one head-line or leads a newscast immediately becomes most important to the news consumer. This assignment of relative significance is a function of the news organization's editorial judgment.

Suppose, for instance, the president makes a speech covering issues A, B, and C, and he considers A the most important; but the wire services and the networks decide to emphasize B or C instead of A. As a news consumer, you are likely to attach importance according to the presentation by the news media; you might never learn of the president's priorities.

If even the president can occasionally run into this problem, consider the plight of the lesser-rank politician with little or no direct access to the public-at-large. The pol is almost entirely at the mercy of the news media's evaluation of the relative importance of what he or she has to say.

The "Screening Process"

The typical presidential campaign begins at least a year before the election, and in the early months at least a half dozen candidates emerge.

If you're like most voters, you like your politics in short doses; you probably respond to a lengthy campaign simply by ignoring most of it. The news media, however, feel compelled to cover the campaign exhaustively, even when the number of candidates and amount of campaign activity are soon greater than the press' ability and desire to cover them.

If, for instance, six presidential candidates are campaigning in Iowa on a given day in January, it is unlikely that the network news-casts will cover each of them. The newscasts would be smothered by politics if equal coverage was given to each candidate. Similarly in the print media, not every candidate can expect front page coverage.

Value judgments by the news media determine who gets covered, how much coverage he gets, and how that coverage is played. In other words, which candidate gets a two-minute story on CBS, which gets 15 seconds? Which candidate's day is reported on page one, which ends up on page 42?

Because the public is unlikely to delve very deeply into campaign news, especially in the early months, the prominence of coverage is crucial. Those candidates receiving the most exposure are likely to be the only ones to catch the voters' eyes. As the candidates compete to win funds and volunteers as well as votes, this visibility is invaluable.

Who receives the most extensive coverage? That is entirely a matter of the press' discretion. A "screening process" operates throughout the campaign as editors, producers, and reporters decide who merits coverage.

This merit generally is based on several factors; how much money a candidate has raised; his standings in the polls; and, reporters' judgments about how effective the candidate's campaign organization is.

Of course, a "Catch 22" operates in this process. A candidate often can't raise money or do well in the polls unless he receives press coverage, but he doesn't receive press coverage unless he has funding and shows up well in the polls.

Press power to shape the destiny of candidates is a source of constant irritation to politicians. Defeated candidates increasingly blame their downfalls on the press—not on biased reporting, but on what might be called a "bias of exclusion" that limits the voters' view of the candidate's efforts.

John Connally, when dropping out of his 1980 quest for the Republican presidential nomination after spending over $12 million and capturing only one delegate, said the press "wrote my obituary long ago" by only occasionally covering his campaign and relegating that coverage to the back pages of publications and short air time on radio and television.

In 1984, Ernest Hollings voiced much the same complaint when he dropped out of the Democratic presidential race. Hollings said that the press had decided to cover a Walter Mondale versus John Glenn race, excluding other candidates.

Even after Gary Hart's upset victories over Mondale proved the press' judgment to be less than perfect, Hollings, Reubin Askew, and Alan Cranston were treated as political lepers.

Reporters defended their coverage decisions in several ways. First, they noted that time and space constraints wouldn't allow them to cover everyone, so they had to decide who the frontrunners were and concentrate on them. This decision, said reporters, was a judgment call, but it was one that they as experienced political journalists felt qualified to make.

The counter-argument that Hollings, for instance, probably would make runs as follows: Suppose those journalists had given Hollings the same exposure Glenn received. And suppose Hollings had mounted a better organized campaign than Glenn was able to muster. And further suppose that Hollings inherently was a more capable potential president than Glenn. Would, then, that coverage have given voters a close enough look at Hollings to ensure the South Carolina senator a reasonable chance to beat frontrunner Mondale? How might the voter have reacted if more had been reported about Hollings' candidacy? Might he have thought more about supporting Hollings?

All this is highly speculative, piling hypothesis upon hypothesis, but the argument underscores several important facts of political life.

First, candidates recognize that news coverage, particularly on television, is essential in making their names known to the voters. Also, the amount of coverage a candidate receives is at least subconsciously perceived by voters as an indication of how seriously a campaign should be taken.

When the press picks the "frontrunners" early in a campaign, this significantly alters political strategy. A candidate must make a strong showing early and capture the press' attention. Waiting until late primaries to make a concerted attack on your opponents might make good sense in terms of strategic campaign theory. But if you wait, by the time you are ready to make your move, the press might have already written you off.

This was part of John Connally's problem in 1980. He had hoped that Ronald Reagan would burn out early in the primaries, perhaps downed by someone such as Tennessee Senator Howard Baker, and then Connally could assume the conservative mantle in the mid-season southern primaries and press on to victory at the convention.

Instead, George Bush bet everything on a strong showing in the first round of political activity, the Iowa caucuses. When he upset Reagan there, the press focused on the Bush-Reagan struggle for the rest of the campaign, forgetting Connally and everyone else.

In 1984, Gary Hart followed a Bush-like strategy, running a good race in Iowa and upsetting Walter Mondale in the second contest in New Hampshire.

The press likes to establish the odds for the campaign horse race early, so if you don't run in the early heats you are likely to be forgotten.

Politicians complain loudly about this screening process, but the news media show no signs of relinquishing their role as arbiters of campaign viability.

The candidates know the rewards of being among those designated as "substantive" by the press. Voters who don't want to be bothered by a careful continuing study of politics look to the news media for guidance about which candidates have the best chance of winning.

This quickly translates into cash for the candidates. Appearing on the cover of *Time* or *Newsweek* as a "frontrunner" can be worth tens of thousands of dollars in campaign contributions. Many donors of campaign money want their dollars going only to candidates who have a chance of winning. (Backing a loser might be altruistic, but relatively few persons make political contributions solely for idealistic reasons.)

Among rank-and-file voters exists a similar predisposition in favor of the candidates who have reasonable chances of winning. Contributors don't like to throw away their money, and most voters want their ballots to go where they are likely to do some good.

Particularly in the early stages of a campaign, when only the true political junkies are paying close attention to the polls and politicians' pronouncements, the news media are relied upon to define the breadth of the field of reasonable choices for the voters.

Occasionally, politicians break through this process, emerging as major contenders even if neglected by the press. At the outset of the contest for the Democratic presidential nomination in 1984, for example, most reporters said the race was Walter Mondale versus John Glenn; everyone else was insignificant or a curiosity.

Gary Hart's campaign—particularly his fund raising—was damaged by this, but Hart's campaign organization was well enough constructed that he was able to run a credible second in Iowa and win a major upset in New Hampshire.

Hart's early efforts were aided considerably by Mondale's overconfidence and Glenn's ineptitude. The lesson of Hart's emergence as a major candidate is that being ignored by the press *can* be overcome, but only if the campaign recognizes that it is laboring under a handicap that press negativism imposes.

Also, the move must be made early. If Hart had delayed (as Connally did in 1980), either Glenn would have survived or some other candidate would have emerged as Mondale's principal rival.

Hart's early victories and his commensurate press coverage were followed closely by a flood of campaign contributions and a dramatic surge in the public opinion polls. As Hart swept through New England and was acclaimed by the press as a political miracle worker, voters throughout the country started paying attention to him.

On the list of candidates worth consideration by voters—a list generated implicitly by the press—Hart suddenly appeared near the top, displacing Glenn and overshadowing everyone else except Mondale. Although they were wrong in their early predictions about a Mondale-Glenn contest, the news media never missed a step; they adjusted their agenda and the public followed along.

Hart's success is the exception rather than the rule. The impact of the press' screening process is even more pronounced in state and local elections in which coverage might be less constant and a candidate whose chances aren't rated high by the press can soon drop from view.

From a candidate's standpoint, it is important to remember that a kind of sliding scale operates: the less coverage offered by the press, the more the campaign itself must compensate through superb organization or heavy spending.

Just as news coverage helps shape the voters' evaluation of candidates, so too does it influence public perception of what issues are important. A good example of this was the coverage of the mid-1980s famine in Ethiopia. Mass starvation is something Americans usually cannot even comprehend; hunger is so foreign to our experience that descriptions of it rarely pierce our naivete.

Television, however, can shatter our insulation. Video of thousands of starving children can so horrify us that "starvation" becomes real to us, rather than remaining merely an abstraction. Only the most skilled writers can convey the tragedy of hunger through their words as effectively as television can through its pictures.

In 1984, a television news team by chance came upon a refugee camp in Ethiopia and recorded on videotape the horrors of death from starvation. When this footage was shown on American television, the outpouring of charitable support for the famine victims was enormous. Newspaper and magazine reports had described the same horrors, but not until the pictures appeared on television was public opinion truly galvanized.

Domestic political issues also may be perceived differently when seen through television's eye. The game of "What if . . . ?" can be played when thinking about how recent history would be different absent the influence of television. For instance, consider the American civil rights movement. Building through the late 1950s and reaching its peak in the early 1960s, this political force might never have achieved its remarkable moral impact had not television conveyed certain images to the millions of Americans who hadn't been stirred or even touched by the movement.

Young black children being led to school through crowds of taunting whites; police dogs attacking non-violent demonstrators; brutishly defiant deputies laughing after being accused of murdering a civil rights worker; Martin Luther King, Jr., describing his dream. *Seeing* these events made civil rights less an esoteric issue and more a dramatic reality.

This was especially true for many northern whites who thought themselves safely distanced from the injustices they might vaguely acknowledge were happening in the south. Reality was suddenly as close as the electronic box in the living room, and this reality had a galvanizing effect, helping to transform civil rights from a purely southern concern into an issue of national morality.

The concept of nationhood, often so nebulous, makes more sense when a common recognition and understanding of issues can be fostered. Television helps do just that. The notion of the world as a "global village" that is unified by communications technology is rapidly becoming reality. At the forefront of that technological evolution, the United States is in many ways already a "national village." Television helped make the civil rights movement (and other events and issues) as real to the resident of Boise, Idaho, as it was to the citizen of Birmingham, Alabama. It became everyone's issue.

Television's pictures don't accomplish this by themselves. Rather, the video stimulates a dialectic process, feeding visual information to the individual viewer, who then uses what he or she has received to conceive and refine opinions. Dramatic pictures can give the brain a jump-start and then accelerate the opinion-formation process. Video is a tool that enhances the news.

Mutual Reliance

The screening process provides a good example of the mutual dependence existing between press and politicians. The pols depend on reporters to make the public aware of candidacies, and the reporters depend on candidates to generate newsworthy material in which the public will be interested.

This tri-partite relationship features continuing give-and-take among public, press, and politicians.

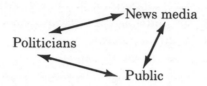

The politicians must communicate directly with the public in order to win votes, and they must respond to the public's interests in particular issues and personalities. The pols, however, also know they must rely heavily on the news media to communicate news about the campaign to the public. And, of course, the pols are dependent on the news media's decisions regarding which candidates deserve coverage.

The flow from public *to* news media is often more difficult to understand. The news business is a commercial enterprise. Publishers and station managers are constantly analyzing subscription figures and ratings to determine if the public is getting the news it wants.

Journalists often hear their editors or producers say, "The public is tired of politics; they want more cops and robbers stories." If this became policy and political coverage was cut back, the entire three-way system would need to be redefined. The candidates would have to be more self-reliant in reaching the voters and the press would become less of a factor. But this would be complicated because the editor's pronouncement that "the public is tired of politics" would quickly become something of a self-fulfilling prophecy.

If the public receives less political information from the news media, voters' interest in the campaign would diminish. Try as they might, the candidates would be hard-pressed to stir up enthusiasm if the principal sources of public information—the news media—didn't stimulate political curiosity.

Economic Factors

Appreciating the economic imperatives of the news business is crucial to understanding the news media's decision-making processes.

News organizations make their money from advertisers. Advertising rates are determined by the number of persons the news entity reaches, as measured by broadcast ratings or print circulation data.

For a network newscast, a single rating point can be worth many millions of dollars in advertising revenues in a year's time. That is why anchormen command astronomical salaries.

This is also the reason there is no such thing as a pure "news judgment" governing what is to be covered and how the coverage will look. All news organizations are in keen competition for readers, listeners, or viewers, and that competition dictates the overall shape of the news that reaches the public.

For example, a presidential candidate might give an important speech on reforming the income tax system. Such a proposal, as significant as it might be, is likely to be laden with complicated statistics and economic theory. A news story—particularly a broadcast story—will be difficult to construct in a way that will interest the average citizen.

If an appealing presentation can't be devised, the story is likely to receive less coverage—an item on the back page of a newspaper, a brief mention by an anchorperson, or perhaps the story will be killed altogether.

On the other hand, if the candidate spends his time participating in events that have less intellectual substance but generate "good pictures" and short, clever quotes, coverage can be more easily obtained.

Such decisions are based on a combination of quantitative information, such as circulation figures, broadcast ratings, and news executives' intuitive feelings about what the public wants. The unfortunate temptation is to drop to the lowest common denominator, gearing coverage to the appetites of "Joe Sixpack," who pays attention to the news only so long as he finds it as entertaining as his favorite TV game show.

News coverage, of course, hasn't become the equivalent of the mindless blather of a game show or a romance novel, but neither does it consistently address the most important issues regardless of their perceived audience appeal.

This means that the political agenda is not only set largely by the news media, but is also governed to a considerable extent by the economic demands of the news business.

In 1987, when financial concerns dictated budget cutbacks in network news operations, the extravagance of some political coverage was questioned. With the money flow drying up, news professionals had to wean themselves from a "more is better" philosophy and decide how much political news the voter truly *needed* and then determine how to ensure that this need was met. This redefinition of the scope of political coverage will probably continue into the 1990s.

Power, profits, agenda-setting. All these are matters that could readily lend themselves to abuse. Little evidence exists, however, of such abuse. One of the marvels of the American press-politics relationship is that it flourishes with so few formal constraints. Somewhere between cooperation and manipulation is the philosophy that guides the symbiotic linkage between news media and politicians.

2 | The "Fourth Branch of Government"

Within days after seizing power in Nicaragua in 1979, the Sandinistas began publishing their own national newspaper, *Barricada*. They used the paper to convey their new government's edicts and propaganda. This move was promptly followed by the establishment of editorial control over the nation's two television channels via the Sandinista Television System.

In addition to creating favorable news organizations, the Sandinistas recognized that opposition media could cause problems. Censorship was imposed on the leading anti-Sandinista newspaper, *La Prensa*, and a church broadcasting station, Radio Catolica. Eventually, even censorship was adjudged by the Sandinistas to be inadequate and the newspaper and station were shut down. Then, in 1987, in an effort to improve world opinion of their regime, the Sandinistas announced they were allowing the two operations to reopen.

This aspect of the Nicaraguan experience is by no means unique. The Sandinistas censoring and then closing the newspaper and station illustrates just how well government leaders understand that the power exercised by opposition media can be far more troublesome than the speeches of individual opposition politicians. Controlling the sources of public information is a fundamental political necessity, whether attained through the malign methods of

17

the Sandinistas or as a result of the assiduous courtship and more temperate manipulation that American politicians employ.

Try to imagine a government without a way to disseminate news; it couldn't exist. Without the American press system as we know it, the government would have to invent its own news media, not unlike *Pravda*, the Communist Party newspaper in the Soviet Union. Any government, be it democratic or totalitarian, must have a way to inform (or give orders to) its people.

To understand the news media's coverage of politics one must understand the power of the press in society, particularly in terms of the press' role as the linking mechanism between government and citizens.

The notion of the American press as the "fourth branch of government" evolved not from any specific Constitutional mandate, but rather from a realistic appraisal of press power. Duties of the executive, legislative, and judicial branches are precisely defined by the Constitution, while the press is more free-floating, left to shape its own role. Accorded sweeping protection by the First Amendment, the news media are free to decide what issues merit coverage, to police governmental performance, and generally to tell the American public what matters they need to pay attention to.

The news media function as a de facto part of the governmental process simply in their basic communication function, telling the public what the president said today, what bills the congress is debating this week, or what decisions the courts made.

Ideally, the press should be self-policing, exercising responsibility commensurate with its power. Of course, wherever power exists, the potential for its abuse exists as well. For the most part, however, the news media act responsibly, if not always the way press critics (especially those in government) would like.

Exercising Press Independence

At the time of the earliest revelations involving the Iran-contra scandal, much of the public seemed to adopt a "Who cares?" attitude or a pro-Reagan, anti-press stance, apparently believing (as some of Reagan's defenders put it) that "the press is out to get another president."

But as news reports continued and formal government investigations began, the scope of the scandal became clear. Live broadcasts of congressional hearings plus extensive reporting kept the matter high on the public agenda. Once again, the news media, although possessing no enforceable power to resolve the issue, kept it in the open and prevented the Reagan administration from sweeping it under the rug.

Similarly, when the government was proving loathe to investigate the Watergate break-in, the press independently began its own investigation of alleged wrongdoing within the executive branch. Not only did the news media directly provide the public with their findings, but their reporting also stimulated the legislative and judicial inquiries that eventually led to President Nixon's resignation.

Charges that the press "drove Nixon from office" are overstatements. The press isn't that powerful; it has no authority to prosecute or even issue subpoenas, much less to force a president to resign. But when the established branches of government fail to respond, this "fourth branch" can keep an issue alive, stimulating public demands for official action.

Publication of the Pentagon Papers in 1971 was a spectacular incidence of reporting that gave lie to the government's official versions of the progress of the Vietnam War. But beyond such well known headline stories, it was day-in, day-out independent news reporting that superceded the government's claims. Most Americans came to rely more heavily on the press than on the government as the most believable source of news about the war.

Foreign policy in this case was not dictated by the news media; again, the press doesn't possess that kind of power. Official policy, however, did have to respond to a public that was greatly influenced by news coverage.

The Vietnam War, as mentioned earlier, was the first war to receive extensive television coverage. President Lyndon Johnson found himself overmatched by television in his struggle for the hearts and minds of the American people. His "rally 'round the flag" exhortations proved inadequate in wooing Americans who had seen—via television—the reality of the war, and who had heard—from the television anchorman—reports contradicting the President's claims.

The most frequently cited example of president-versus-anchor-man face-off occurred in 1968, when CBS anchorman Walter Cronkite included in his report of his trip to Vietnam this damning prognosis: "It seems now more certain than ever that the bloody experience of Vietnam is to end in a stalemate. . . . To say that we are closer to victory today is to believe, in the face of the evidence, the optimists who have been wrong in the past. . . . It is increasingly clear to this reporter that the only rational way out . . . will be to negotiate, not as victors but as an honorable people who lived up to their pledge to defend democracy and did the best they could."

After this broadcast, Johnson reportedly told some of his senior staff members that if he had lost Cronkite, he had lost the nation.

That statement has the ring of Johnsonian overstatement. Certainly the President was feeling beleaguered in those days after the Vietnamese communists' Tet offensive. Shortly thereafter, Johnson announced he would not seek another term as president. It is hard to believe, however, that a politician as tough and skillful as Lyndon Johnson would throw in the towel solely because of a journalist's pronouncements.

Hypotheses about Johnson's psyche aren't needed here, but the President's acknowledgement of the news anchor's role in shaping public opinion is instructive. Johnson's experience raises some issues about how television affects presidential decision-making.

Policy makers must take into consideration the impact of the visual image conveyed by television. Austin Ranney of the American Enterprise Institute offered this bit of historical speculation: "If there had been live coverage of the Civil War, it would have ended in 1862 with the establishment of the Confederacy because it was a terribly bloody war and the North was losing most of the early part of it."

Lyndon Johnson raised the same issue in a speech to the National Association of Broadcasters shortly after he decided not to run. He asked rhetorical questions about whether Americans, during the latter stages of World War II, would have been willing to continue supporting the policy of seeking unconditional surrender from Hitler if television had provided daily coverage of the Germans' counter-attacks during the Battle of the Bulge.

Such matters are the stuff of interesting speculation, but more importantly, to what extent does the prospect of television coverage constrain a president's use of military power? Would President Reagan have yielded to the temptation to intervene directly in Nicaragua if he didn't have to worry about nightly television pictures of American soldiers killed or wounded in pursuit of a questionable policy goal? Will future presidents have to forsake the "limited war" option because of the difficulty of maintaining public support for such ventures in the age of virtually instantaneous coverage?

On the one hand, television performs a noble function if it helps keep the United States out of future Vietnams. On the other, given the unfortunate realities of geopolitics, might "limited war" sometimes be unavoidable in halting a skid towards a major war? These are difficult questions. Certainly the ideal would be to fight no war at all. But the ideal isn't always an option.

Heads of state have shown that they recognize the constraints news coverage can impose. When President Reagan ordered the landings in Grenada in 1983, news coverage was carefully blocked until the administration decided to allow it. The stated reason was to preserve the secrecy of the attack, but certainly, ranking members of the administration had to fear the potential backlash if the enterprise didn't go well and Americans were treated to pictures of U.S. forces being shot down on the beaches of a country few people had even heard of.

Similarly, British Prime Minister Margaret Thatcher tightly controlled coverage of the Falklands War of 1982. Initially, public enthusiasm for a costly war to recover distant islands was limited, and Thatcher didn't want to run the political risk of being second-guessed while the war was getting underway.

By limiting news coverage, Thatcher was able to control not the substance of news reports but the timing of them, and could present the British public with something of a fait accompli. She could retain her ability to lead public opinion rather than letting news coverage take that power away from her.

Issues of war and peace aren't the only matters that have been affected by the increasing speed and intensity of news coverage. Virtually every facet of government and politics reflects in some way the demands of the news business. Sometimes the quest for news stories creates a "fast-forward effect." In essence, this is a compression of the time, and thus a limitation on the options, policy makers have for reaching decisions.

People are used to getting news quickly and in small, terse doses. Particularly for those persons who rely heavily on television, complex issues are seen in simplified form and the whole world seems to operate in synch with the deadlines of daily newscasts. Policy makers must either keep up with this pace or risk public displeasure.

That is partly a by-product of a television-oriented culture. After all, if Bill Cosby can resolve any problem within 30 minutes, the government should be able to do likewise. The analogy between situation comedy and government is a tempting one, but—for good or ill—Cosby's scriptwriters don't govern the world.

Similarly, if Tom Brokaw needs no more than two minutes to give us a report on a complex topic such as federal tax policy, why shouldn't the president be able to explain his policies just as concisely? Again, that's not how the world works, but perhaps a yearning for simplicity has overwhelmed logic.

In such instances, is the tail wagging the dog? That certainly must be the feeling of the frustrated government official who finds his work being prematurely unveiled to the public just to satisfy an insatiable news appetite.

Sometimes this pressure can be beneficial, pushing the bureaucracy forward and keeping government from falling victim to inertia. On other occasions, however, the "fast-forward effect" can be a factor in imprudent decision-making.

For example, to what extent did news coverage of the Iran hostage situation in 1980—coverage that was assumed to be fueling public impatience—influence President Carter's decision to launch the ill-fated rescue attempt? Because it is so brisk and so oriented to bringing a "story" to its conclusion, news coverage often seems to be sending a subliminal message to public and government alike: "Hurry up, hurry up."

Furthermore, would the hostages have been as big an issue if the news media had not lavished such coverage on the event?

Walter Cronkite ended each evening's CBS newscast with, "And that's the way it is, on this the — day of Americans being held hostage in Iran." ABC presented a nightly special, "America Held Hostage, Day —," that was the precursor of "Nightline."

The indignation implicit in these daily litanies almost certainly heightened Americans' dissatisfaction with President Carter's handling of the crisis and worked to the advantage of Carter's challenger, Ronald Reagan.

If the news media had taken a more low key approach to the hostage situation, covering it like other continuing stories, the issues might not have seemed as hot to most voters. Diplomacy might have proceeded more effectively out of the ubiquitous glare of the media's spotlight, and Carter might have been able to free his campaign from being held hostage by this single issue.

Of course, the White House exacerbated the situation by making so obvious its absorption with this issue. Early in the crisis, Carter declared that he would not leave the White House to campaign until the hostages were freed.

Carter later had to renege on this pledge, but by staking his presidency on his ability to resolve the hostage situation, he had invited press and public to attach the greatest importance to the matter. This roll of the dice turned out to be a major factor in Carter's November defeat.

Some people sympathetic to Carter's plight blame the news media for making a bad situation worse, arguing that coverage was overdone and forced Carter to undertake some imprudent actions, such as the disastrous rescue attempt. Certainly, a president trying to resolve a complex situation has enough to worry about in terms of deciding what intelligence data to believe, how to involve foreign allies, how to balance conflicting advice from his staff and cabinet, and other such matters. News coverage might seem a nuisance at best, or a serious obstruction at worst.

But what is the alternative—a total blackout of coverage? White House staff members might like that, but journalists aren't in the business of pleasing government officials. A president's ability or inability to resolve difficult crises is something the public has a right to know about. Granted, the news spotlight doesn't make the president's job any easier in such cases, but the democratic system would be dangerously undermined if that spotlight could be turned on and off according to White House whim.

Carter's Iran hostage problem wasn't an isolated case. Securing the release of captives—regardless of a president's involvement—has increasingly involved media-related issues. The international epidemic of hostage-taking has raised a variety of questions about the role the news media should and do play.

Consider this scenario: A commercial passenger airplane is hi-jacked over Europe and taken to Beirut. The hijackers, members of a radical Moslem sect, demand political concessions and cash. Fifty American passengers are removed from the plane and taken to an undisclosed location in Beirut. The American government offers to negotiate to obtain its citizens' release.

How should this be covered? First, it's a major news story, so blacking out coverage is not a realistic option, even if U.S. officials claim their negotiations would proceed more smoothly absent the pressures generated by aroused public opinion. So representatives of the print and electronic media descend on Beirut.

When they arrive, they are greeted by press representatives of the hostage-takers. The reporters are handed news releases detail-ing the captors' demands and invitations to a news conference fea-turing selected hostages. Also, the hijackers' press agents let it be known that exclusive interviews with individual hostages or leaders of the hijackers can be arranged for substantial fees.

Meanwhile back home, camera crews have camped out on the front yards of families of the hostages, ready to ask family members "How do you feel?" about the situation. In Washington, White House press secretaries are being barraged with questions about the president's mood and his likely response to the hijackers' de-mands.

This not-so-hypothetical case illustrates some of the pitfalls that await journalists pursuing such a story. Even terrorists know how to manipulate the media, so the question, "Who's in charge?" can be as pertinent to a hostage crisis as it is to a political campaign.

News organizations must keep control of their media. Television and radio are in a particularly precarious situation. By agreeing to broadcast the hijackers' news conference—especially if live—control of the airwaves is effectively being surrendered. Buying interviews in such a case is "checkbook journalism" at its worst. This is more than aggressive reporting; it is subsidizing terrorism.

Interviews with hostages' families quickly cross the line into overkill. Aside from the invasions of privacy and the soap opera tone that such interviews often include, little real news is likely to be obtained.

Pressuring the White House for comment is a far different mat-ter, but the realities of diplomacy are such that only a terribly naive reporter will expect full disclosure about what is happening. Even if a correspondent digs up some good information, such as a report about troop movements that are part of a hostage rescue plan, publishing such news prematurely would be irresponsible, endangering the lives of hostages and soldiers.

All these matters indicate that the search for news cannot be an unrestrained, headlong pursuit. Judgment about impact has to be a factor in editorial decision-making. During the hijacking of a TWA plane in 1985, news judgment sometimes seemed lacking and press behavior was occasionally out of control.

For example, at a news conference arranged by the hijackers, some reporters became so unruly that the terrorists had to fire their weapons in the air to restore order. A certain black humor might be found in seeing the hijackers meeting their anarchic match in the form of the press corps, but journalism inevitably will not function well in such chaos.

In July, 1985, after the TWA hostages had been released, *Newsweek's* Jonathan Alter offered a thoughtful list of suggestions that might help television journalists avoid such media circus performances:

• Pool raw footage of hostages and terrorists to end unseemly competition for exclusives. Network representatives trying to curry favor with hijackers through bribes or other deals will certainly undermine public faith in all news organizations.

• Avoid live or unedited coverage, because such broadcasts tend to take control of the airwaves away from the journalists and put it in the hands of the terrorists.

• Limit coverage of hostages' families to material that satisfies genuine information needs rather than mere morbid curiosity.

• Resist interrupting regular programming with overly dramatic bulletins that sometimes turn out to be little more than showcases for an anchor's ego. Crawl lines across the bottom of the screen are adequate to keep viewers informed of less-than-momentous developments.

• Recognize that hostages are just that, and cannot be expected to speak freely even if made available to reporters by their captors. Therefore, if a journalist decides to interview a hostage, questions should be phrased carefully and potentially dangerous political issues should not be raised.

• Avoid covering "media events" staged by terrorists. By definition, hostage-takers are adversaries of a system that allows free
exchanges of ideas, so nothing is gained by giving them unrestricted
access to media channels. News organizations should be selective in
what they cover.

Alter's suggestions are a good starting point for the development
of guidelines that news organizations could implement. As in other
aspects of covering government and politics, the news media must
recognize how powerful they are. In a hostage situation, as in a
political campaign, news coverage can affect the outcome.

Given the obvious tension that exists in the relationship between
news media and government, you might think true enmity breeds
irresponsible behavior by both sides. Critics who say that the news
business is devoid of ethics and consciously disregards the nation's
best interests generally are mistaken.

Press independence does not require abandonment of patriotic
conscience. For instance, major news organizations rarely plunge
into publicly disclosing matters that will endanger national security. Journalists don't ask government officials for permission to
publish a story, but they often will let those officials make their
arguments against publication, and, if the appropriate editors or
producers think the government's case has merit, they are likely to
delete all or parts of a pending story.

Good examples of how this process works are provided in Bob
Woodward's 1987 best-seller, *Veil*, a history of the CIA during the
Reagan administration. Woodward recounts lengthy negotiations
between the *Washington Post* and administration officials regarding the *Post's* plans to run a story about the secrets an American
intelligence employee had sold to the Soviet Union. CIA Director
William Casey and other foreign policy planners feared that such
publication would tell the Soviets more than they already knew
and confirm the seriousness of the damage the spy had done.

According to Woodward, Casey talked with the *Post's* executive
editor, Ben Bradlee, 20 times during six months of discussions about
the story. President Reagan called *Post* board chairman Katherine
Graham to ask her to be particularly careful with the story. Various
intelligence officials were queried not only about the substance of

the story but also about the effect it might have on the intelligence-gathering competition between the United States and the Soviet Union. All this time, the *Post* sat on the story, willing to accept, at least temporarily, the administration's argument that national security would be harmed by the information Woodward and other reporters had dug up.

Throughout these negotiations, Woodward and his colleagues had to be careful that they didn't become too cooperative with the government. After all, their obligation to the public couldn't be foresaken simply because administration officials might become unhappy. A constant worry was about the candor of Casey and others. Was national security really in jeopardy, or were the politicians simply using that claim as a smokescreen to justify their penchant for secrecy?

The delicate process took an ugly turn when Casey threatened federal prosecution if the *Post* or anyone else published certain of the material in question. Despite this provocation, the *Post* continued to proceed with great caution. Finally, when the spy's trial began and other news organizations began publishing stories about what intelligence operations had been compromised, the *Post* went ahead with an abbreviated version of the original article.

Several lessons emerge from this case. First, communication can and does take place between the news media and government. The *Washington Post* and the Reagan administration might seem unlikely partners in such a process, but they made it work, regardless of mutual distrust and tensions. Second, the *Post's* actions indicate that reporters and editors aren't always so intent on rushing a story into print that they ignore the effect the story can have. The nation's interests *do* matter to responsible journalists.

Journalists have mixed feelings about their "fourth branch" identity. Most journalists relish their power (even if they are hesitant to admit it) because they like to see their work have some effect. At the same time, conscientious journalists know they must not slip into the roles of the persons and institutions about which they report.

The "fourth branch" notion is ethically acceptable if developed in the context of the press as the public's surrogate. In this role—as investigator, interlocutor, explainer—the press can perform as both active and passive participant in the political process, not setting policy or forcing outcomes, but directing attention to policy options and illuminating possible outcomes of those policies.

When all is said and done, the press generally welcomes a certain level of tension in its relationship with politicians. An adversary tone keeps both sides sharp and is a reasonably good guarantee that the public will receive a full and accurate account of political news.

So when you watch Sam Donaldson and his colleagues working over a politician, remember this isn't being done out of spite. Such verbal rough-housing is, for the moment, state-of-the-art news gathering.

News media and government have to coexist. Though Lyndon Johnson threw up his hands and said he'd had enough, few politicians go that far. A certain parity exists between the two powerful forces. The system as a whole, despite periods of imbalance, generally returns to equilibrium.

3 | News Media and Politicians— Who's in Charge?

If you voted for Ronald Reagan in 1984, did you vote for the Republican candidate for president, who happened to be Ronald Reagan, or did you vote for Ronald Reagan, who happened to be the Republican candidate?

In many respects, the rise in media influence has been both a product of and contributor to the decline in political parties' fortunes. Especially when making their choices at the top of the ballot, voters may tend to pay less attention to party label and more to the individual candidate.

The news media have enhanced the personality-oriented approach to electoral decision-making. Now voters, through the media, get a good look at many of the candidates, rather than arriving at the election day polling place with little to base selections on beyond the candidates' party affiliations.

The flood of political reporting also makes it easy for voters to rely on the press, rather than on the parties, as the principal source of information about candidates and issues.

As party significance declines and voters pay less attention to party labels, split-ticket voting becomes more common. Candidates react to this by worrying less about their identification with a party, concentrating instead on using the news media as the principal channel to the electorate.

This process develops its own momentum. While politicians depend increasingly on news media rather than traditional partisan resources, the power of parties continues to slip and, in turn, the importance of the press grows to fill whatever vacuum might exist.

Newspersons recognize their increasing power and sometimes they flaunt it. Too often the press' attitude towards a candidate seems to be, "You need us more than we need you, so make certain your campaign events and schedules conform to our needs and deadlines or we'll ignore you and no voter will ever hear of you."

Particularly those candidates you find at the lower end of the ballot (in local judicial races, for example) so desperately want a rare bit of news coverage that they aren't above drastically reshaping campaign schedules to attract and accommodate reporters.

And in states or communities in which party organizations are in disrepair, candidates know they must shape their campaigns to meet press needs.

How conscious are voters of this transformation in American politics? Do they dislike or welcome the displacement of parties by news media? Do they notice it?

More often than not, political parties often appear to be organizational dinosaurs, especially to persons who vote only once every four years (pulled to the polls by a presidential race). People have grown accustomed to relying on network reporters, rather than on party workers, as the main source of needed political information.

Yet the parties should and do serve a valuable purpose in the political system, and though their role has changed and their influence has declined, by no means are they dead.

While diverse informational sources have made the parties less crucial in election day decision-making for many voters, parties are still the glue that holds together the policy-shaping process. This is especially true in Congress, which is the logical site for any potential resurgence in party activism. Fundamental philosophical differences still distinguish Democrats and Republicans.

Sometimes, however, weak party leadership allows those distinctions to become fuzzy, and that seems to have been a particular problem in recent years. This is a problem not easily remedied because doing so requires a high level of intellectual energy, something often in short supply in Congress. But it isn't a lost cause. Perhaps the best way to develop a prognosis for the parties is to examine the functions that they can still perform well and that might be the keys to their revitalization.

The goal for party leaders might simply be in answering the voters' most basic question: "Why should I be a Democrat/Republican?" The answer must be more than, "Because we're the party of Franklin Roosevelt/Ronald Reagan."

Political parties have an identity that extends beyond personalities, one that is more substantive than the fine-sounding rhetoric that makes up the party platform approved by delegates at the quadrennial national conventions. Party identity, if it is to have real meaning, must be based on a solid legislative record: the party that raised the minimum wage, the party that led the fight for an arms control treaty, and other such accomplishments that a voter can grab onto.

This reassertion of party leadership has yet to take hold. And so, the trends toward split-ticket voting and "independent" status as opposed to strong traditional party affiliation continue, placing ever greater responsibility on non-partisan providers of political information, such as the news media.

One sound criticism of the press is that news organizations don't always appreciate the significance of their non-partisan role. Reporting cannot be dismissed as a politically passive enterprise; the news (and how it is presented) has a significant impact on how votes are cast.

The public pays attention not only to the substance of reports but also to their tone. The sarcastic metaphors that may enliven a journalist's work can affect public perceptions of the subject of the news story.

That these personal touches are part of "the news" shouldn't surprise anyone. Journalists are human; their work cannot be wholly divorced from feelings that develop in the course of covering a campaign for weeks or even months on end.

Press as Participant

To what extent have the news media become participants in, rather than solely reporters of, the political process?

To use a theater analogy, the politicians perform on a stage before an audience of voters. The press aids the audience, describing what is happening on the stage. In this model, the news media clearly are reporters—interlocutors for the audience—not actors themselves.

But because of the press' growing role in politics, members of the news media may be climbing onto the stage, leaving the audience and joining the ranks of the performers.

Evidence of this transformation abounds. The press decides which candidates are credible, which issues are important, whose campaigns are being well run, which candidacies are worthy of voter consideration, and which might as well be ignored.

In studying what is occurring on stage, the audience of voters thus must not only interpret the actions of the politicians, but they must also evaluate the quality of information the news media are providing.

One bit of tangible evidence of this changing press role is seen in news stories about the nature of political coverage and about the way candidates treat the press. In other words, the press is now covering itself.

For example, before the opening of a national party convention you'll inevitably see stories about how many miles of cable have been used to wire the convention hall, how many reporters are present (and by what ratio they outnumber the delegates), and so forth. The message implicit in such stories is, "The public is lucky the press is here in such a dominant role."

Perhaps so. Such reports, however, rarely explore how the convention process has been reshaped to meet press demands. In fact, the conventions might not still exist in their present form but for the fact that the parties' leaders have figured out how to use the massive amounts of coverage to their advantage as a prolonged political advertisement.

The entire pace of the convention is geared to the exigencies of network television. Speakers vie for scheduling that will give them the opportunity for a prime time appearance. The events the pols want the public to see—such as the nominee's acceptance speech—are scheduled to occur when the television audience is likely to be largest.

This wasn't always the case. During the Democrats' chaotic 1972 convention in Miami Beach, nominee George McGovern wasn't able to mount the rostrum to deliver his major speech (with its eloquent "Come home, America" theme) until after 2:00 A.M. eastern time.

This speech, which many observers thought was the best McGovern ever made, was unseen by most of the nation.

When the Democrats next convened, in 1976 in New York, the convention that nominated Jimmy Carter was rigidly scheduled. Political maneuvering took a back seat to television; Carter's acceptance speech was delivered right on schedule in television's prime time.

For their part, news executives (especially, but not exclusively, those of the television networks) have designed their convention coverage to be in part an extended advertisement for themselves.

Convention week usually offers little important news (since conventions are among the most predictable political events), so the news media concentrate on displaying all their electronic gadgetry and journalistic superstars to a public that rarely is as impressed with the press as the press is with itself.

During day-to-day campaign coverage, news organizations are less likely to promote themselves so overtly, but the role of the press increasingly finds its way into news reports.

For example, during the late stages of the 1980 presidential campaign, when Republican nominee Ronald Reagan virtually eliminated his direct press contacts, a network reporter often inserted in his stories a line such as this: "On this, the 20th straight day the candidate has gone without holding a press conference . . . ."

Justification for this kind of reporting is found in the theory that the press acts as the voters' surrogate. If the press is denied access to the candidate, so this theory goes, then the candidate is removing himself from the reach of the electorate.

The politicians respond that this is nonsense; they can reach the public directly through their campaigns regardless of the extent to which the press' demands are satisfied.

Both sides are partly correct. A candidate is hard to hold accountable if he eliminates all spontaneity from his campaign and is seen by the public principally through advertising created in totally controlled environments (such as ads featuring conversations with the "man on the street" who is actually a carefully rehearsed actor).

Even when a candidate appears at rallies, delivers public speeches, and performs other such campaign duties, he remains in almost total control. These heavily planned events allow him to say what he wants to say, look how he wants to look, and generally present the image of his choice to the voters.

A classic example of this technique was found in Richard Nixon's 1968 presidential campaign. As documented by Joe McGinniss in *The Selling of the President 1968,* the Nixon campaign staff felt that one of the reasons for Nixon's narrow loss to John Kennedy in 1960 had been unfavorable press coverage and negative impressions created by Nixon's television appearances. The byword for the 1968 effort became "control" as press access to the candidate was severely limited and even the most spontaneous-appearing television appearances were meticulously planned.

With a little bit of freedom, the press corps can disrupt this stage-managed approach to campaigning. Reporters can ask questions the candidate might not want to answer, covering issues campaign strategists would prefer to ignore. The press can raise the curtain at odd times, letting the public see what goes on backstage during the campaign.

Candidates and campaign managers respond that the press has no *right* to dictate what deserves coverage and no *right* to demand special access to the candidate. The pols' argument is that the news media's job is to cover what is going on, present this to the public via their news reports, and then let the voters do whatever they want at the polls.

The tug-of-war continues. Reporters clamor for more access to candidates; the pols figure out new ways to tighten their control over the pace and substance of the campaign. The voter watches, understandably skeptical and only sporadically attentive.

Television Power

Looming increasingly large in all these matters is television. This relatively new device, which in a few decades has had profound effect on American life, is considered an omnipotent force by most politicians.

The speed with which television has taken its place in the United States is impressive in itself. As America moved into the post–World War II era, fewer than one out of every one hundred homes had a television set. By 1950, still less than 10 percent of households were tuning in to this new medium. Then came the explosion.

By 1955, two-thirds of homes had televisions. In 1960, the figure had reached 87 percent. Now roughly 98 percent of American households have at least one television set.

That pervasiveness means power, and the speed with which it was attained meant that politics, like many other aspects of American life (such as advertising), had to change rapidly to keep pace. Earlier in the century, radio had had a similar effect, and politicians such as Franklin Roosevelt proved that mastery of this medium could significantly strengthen ties between pol and voters.

The rules of the political game changed again with the advent of television. Just as Roosevelt had made radio work for him, now a new generation of politicians began to explore the ways in which television might help or hurt a candidate's prospects. Today's most successful politicians are those who master the art of appearing "telegenic," just like actors who perform on television. One could argue that with this kind of process Abraham Lincoln could never have been elected president because he looked ungainly and had a squeaky voice.

Regardless of Mr. Lincoln's hypothetical prospects as a television candidate, for good or ill television has imposed new requirements on present-day vote seekers. Among the new criteria by which we judge candidates are the following:

• Physical appearance. Television brings us very close to the candidate. Because we see the politician on the screen, just as we see our favorite actors and actresses, we tend to measure politicians according to standards of sex appeal and other such matters that are more relevant for "stars" than for elected officials. To what extent is a voter's decision based on his feel for the candidate's personality as opposed to more esoteric concerns such as issues positions?

• Ability to use the accoutrements of television: the cameras, teleprompter, lighting, and other gadgetry. Compare, for example, the television performances of Presidents Jimmy Carter and Ronald Reagan. Reagan, the former professional actor, clearly felt comfortable staring into the camera; he was skilled at reading a script and at using the medium to "come into the living room" of his viewer. Carter, on the other hand, rarely seemed at ease on television; he didn't seem to feel he was really talking to anything more than an electronic box. Skill in using television probably is not a determinative measure of presidential competence, but Reagan's political fortunes were aided and Carter's hurt by their respective television skills.

• Ability to adapt to the limits of television news programs. The average story in a national or local television newscast runs less than two minutes. The story usually is composed of many different video and audio segments edited to form a coherent whole. "Sound-bites," the television equivalent of a direct quotation in print, rarely run longer than 20 seconds. Candidates must learn to "speak in soundbites," making their key points in neat phrases that won't have to be cut and sutured by a videotape editor. Of course, many issues don't lend themselves to such quick treatment. The politician thus faces the choice of being superficial or being edited. The former is the safest course. But how much substantive information has the viewer gleaned from such high-speed politics?

These are just some of the ways television shapes a candidacy. Whether seeking the presidency or a minor local office, few candidates totally escape the need to conform to the demands of television.

Presidential Debates

One of the most eventful changes in politics, particularly in presidential races, has been the advent of televised debates between candidates.

Carrying with them their formidable reputation as a crucial testing ground for potential presidents, the national debates apparently affected the outcomes of three of the four elections in which they were held.

In these three races—all of which were closely contested—non-incumbents or underdogs bested their challengers and went on to win the election. (The exception to this pattern was the 1984 debate series between President Ronald Reagan and Democratic challenger Walter Mondale. Although Mondale did well in the two debates, he trailed Reagan so badly that not even the debates could slow the incumbent's momentum.)

John F. Kennedy in the 1960 debates proved he could look as "presidential" as his opponent, Vice President Richard Nixon. In 1976, challenger Jimmy Carter proved he could more than hold his own against President Gerald Ford. In 1980, the tables were turned on President Carter, as his challenger, Ronald Reagan, gave a presidential-level performance.

The first Kennedy-Nixon debate was a major event in the history of television and politics. Kennedy had been accused of being too young and inexperienced to be entrusted with the presidency. During the debate, however, he proved himself at least Nixon's equal. Kennedy was well rested and had been carefully rehearsed; he confidently snapped off his answers while Nixon fidgeted and seemed ill at ease.

The measure of the impact of television as television was found by some post-debate polling. Persons who watched the debate on television thought Kennedy had won; persons who had listened to the debate on radio thought Nixon had prevailed.

Nixon's performance was criticized less for the substance of his answers than for his appearance. Disdaining professional make-up help, Nixon (who had recently been ill) looked as grey as the backdrop of the debate set. Nixon's pallor and his grey suit gave him an aura of drabness, especially in contrast to Kennedy's tanned face and dark suit.

Nixon also used traditional debate style and addressed himself to his opponent, while Kennedy played to the cameras, addressing his remarks directly to the television audience. When the camera showed a cut-away shot of Nixon while Kennedy talked, Nixon looked shifty-eyed and worried. (These unflattering shots of Nixon turned up in Kennedy's television advertising during the rest of the campaign.)

All these matters, of course, have little to do with the conduct of the presidency. The television appearance of candidates, however, appeals to voters' emotions and basic instincts: Who can be most trusted with the presidency?

Many voters' ballot decisions are not based on careful analysis of issues and candidates' backgrounds but on an instinctive feeling for whom they trust and like. Television is a useful tool for this kind of decision-making.

The impact of the 1960 debates scared politicians. Frontrunning candidates found countless reasons why they should not debate (such as an incumbent citing national security reasons for not discussing some issues, and major party candidates refusing to share debate time with a slew of minor party hopefuls).

Not until 1976, when the country was still reeling from the Watergate scandals and candor from candidates was much in demand, was the next presidential debate held. Republican President Gerald Ford debated Jimmy Carter and vice presidential nominees Robert Dole and Walter Mondale met in their own match-up.

Carter faced much the same task as Kennedy had. The former Georgia governor was benefiting from being an outsider, untainted by Washington's evils. But however much they liked the idea of having a different kind of politician in the White House, many voters still weren't certain they wanted to trust the inexperienced Carter rather than the bland but safe Ford.

During the debates, Carter "looked presidential" enough to overcome most of these fears. He also benefited from a Ford gaffe in which the president apparently denigrated the power of the Soviet Union in Eastern Europe.

Ford's slip of the tongue was costly. He spent most of the next week trying to explain what he meant. This derailed his campaign sufficiently to give Carter a needed boost in the close race.

A gaffe such as Ford's Eastern Europe comment is an example of why many politicians worry so much about television. Not only is such an error damaging when first uttered, but television, with its penchant for constant replays of such occurrences, magnifies the impact of the remark.

In the context of a 90-minute debate, a single sentence might not stand out, but when it is isolated and repeated time and time again, the audience ascribes increasing importance to it. By focusing extra attention on such a matter, the press tells the public, "This is important." When this happens, the candidate has no alternative but to treat the issue as being as important as the press (and now the voters) have come to believe it to be.

The 1980 debate between President Carter and Ronald Reagan gave Reagan a chance to prove several things: that he wasn't too old to handle the complex issues a president must address; that he wasn't a right-wing fanatic ready to lob missiles at the Kremlin; and that he could masterfully use television to his political advantage.

Carter's obvious discomfort when facing the cameras enhanced Reagan's appearance as a self-confident, good-natured leader. Reagan's use of humor, his ability to fashion memorable, if inconsequential, phrases ("There you go again"), and his skill in summarizing the theme of his campaign in a few seconds ("Are you better off today than you were four years ago?") all contributed to his success in this debate.

With the passing of four years, Reagan's sharpness in debate diminished. Facing former Vice President Walter Mondale in their first 1984 debate, Reagan looked tired and unprepared. Mondale, whose campaign was so badly lagging that he trailed Reagan by almost 30 points in some polls, seemed the more forceful and competent of the two men in their 90-minute debate.

The press' almost unanimous verdict was that Mondale had "won" this debate and thus, with a month to go before election day, had a chance to resuscitate his campaign. Newscasts for several days following the debate used short clips from the confrontation to focus on Mondale's strength and Reagan's weakness as debaters.

By magnifying these aspects of the debate, news coverage enhanced Mondale's victory. Short excerpts from the debate featured in news stories compressed and reshaped the event, especially for audiences that hadn't seen the debate.

During the debate, the candidates and the panel of reporters questioning them could place emphasis where they chose, indicating through the selection of questions and the substance of answers what they thought most important. In post-debate coverage, however, reporters and editors can take it upon themselves to decide what should be emphasized. Thus, the "new reality" of the debate is defined after the event by the press.

All the analysis and re-analysis by the press turned out to do Mondale little good. The Democrat's campaign made no lasting gains in the polls. In the second debate, Reagan displayed enough of his old finesse to dispel notions that he no longer could handle his job.

This recovery by Reagan underscored one of the weaknesses of both the debate format and the coverage of debates. Probably the best-remembered and most-reported aspect of the second debate was a fairly feeble joke delivered by Reagan when questioned about any effects his age might be having on his ability to do his job.

Nuggets are retained; lengthier deposits of wisdom or foolishness are usually discarded. In this case, Mondale watched haplessly. He knew what was happening and probably regretted that in his professed pursuit of substance he had kept himself from producing those few moments that an audience is most likely to remember.

Mondale certainly could have been proclaimed the "winner" of the second as well as the first debate if scoring had been based on traditional debating points. But it wasn't, and he wasn't able to capitalize on his performance to the extent necessary to offset his other campaign problems.

Contrary to the precedent established by Kennedy, Carter, and Reagan, Mondale was the first non-incumbent or underdog to do well in a televised debate and still lose the election. Of course, none of the three earlier victors had trailed his opponent by such a massive margin prior to debating.

The press may attribute more value to the debates than the public does. The fervor of post-debate reporting is rarely matched by spontaneous post-debate voter interest.

Perhaps the novelty of presidential debates has diminished and voters consider them less of a factor in their electoral decision-making. Perhaps the format—which is more a series of miniature speeches than a true debate—is seen by the voter as lessening the significance of the face-offs. After all, these are only 90-minute segments of a long campaign.

The televised debates, however, have probably become regular elements of our presidential campaigns. That is fine as long as voters keep them in perspective and recognize that they are at least as much television "events" as they are substantive political discourse.

Television is in the vanguard of growing press influence on the political process. As the news media make more information available, voters will be better informed (in theory, at least) when they cast their ballots.

Increasing public reliance on the press means the press must take its job increasingly seriously. The equation is simple: Press influence plus public reliance equals press power. A corollary equation can also be simply stated, but it doesn't always work: Press power produces press responsibility.

The next big test for American news media will be that of addressing the issues raised in these equations. New standards of fairness, more appreciation of how the news business affects Americans, and better understanding of the political process (and the press' impact on it) are among the matters journalists must consider if the symbiotic relationship between news and politics is to remain healthy.

The public is the ultimate referee, deciding if the balance of power is being maintained properly. When an individual watches coverage of campaigns, he must impose his own standards of fairness and intellectual honesty on what he is seeing.

4 | On the Bus— The Press' Perspective

Consider the following actual day's schedule of a reporter covering the 1980 campaign when Ronald Reagan was still fighting George Bush for the nomination. This was a day of campaigning in Texas only (a relatively rare one-state day).

6:30 A.M.: San Antonio (after arrival at hotel at 11:00 P.M. the preceding night): press luggage must be in lobby for Secret Service inspection and transfer to airport.

7:00: press gathers at back of hotel and boards flotilla of boats on San Antonio River for 20-minute trip with Reagan from hotel to convention center. This trip would take three minutes by automobile, but the river trip offers better video opportunities.

8:00: Reagan addresses Mexican-American group. Crowd response is luke-warm. Reporters would like to interview members of the audience after the candidate's speech, but the schedule doesn't allow this. The press must be at the motorcade ready to roll by the time Reagan reaches his car, so reporters and cameramen rush to the buses and ignore the audience.

8:30–10:00: several more San Antonio events, all designed to generate "pretty pictures" for television and all keeping Reagan well removed from direct contact with voters and reporters.

10:15: depart San Antonio.

10:45: arrive Harlingen; high school bands, flag-waving children, and former Dallas Cowboys quarterback Roger Staubach greet Reagan; motorcade to center of town.

11:45: motorcade and platform delays push Reagan's scheduled 11:00 speech back to 11:45. The speech covers Reagan's policy on illegal immigration and apparently takes issue with Texas' Republican governor's views on the same topic. But Reagan and his key staff members are nowhere to be found after the speech; they have gone to private meetings with local politicians.

12:30–12:45: lunch. Scheduling problems have cut the planned 45 minutes for lunch to 15 minutes. The press corps descends on a restaurant where the campaign staff has had telephones temporarily installed for reporters' story filing needs. Some reporters stand in line to contact their editors and producers; some television and radio reporters find broom closets or other relatively quiet places to tape the narrations for their stories. No one gets any food.

1:00: depart Harlingen.

1:20: arrive Corpus Christi; high school bands, flag-waving children, and Roger Staubach once again perform. Television crews toss bags of videotapes over a fence to waiting couriers who will take them to a nearby microwave transmitter to be fed to stations for early evening newscasts. Reagan gives standard campaign speech; nothing new.

2:00: depart Corpus Christi.

2:30: arrive Beaumont; another airport rally, nothing new.

3:15: depart Beaumont.

3:30: arrive Houston.

3:45: motorcade from Houston airport to center of city. Reagan greeted by cheering campaign volunteers at hotel where he (and press corps) will spend the night. Reagan is whisked to his suite. Reporters check in, call editors and finish stories about day's activity.

5:00: press departs for convention center, site of major fundraising dinner for Reagan. Reporters set up in roped-off areas and are ordered away by ushers when trying to interview dinner guests. Reporters then settle back to watch rich people eat their dinners and listen to Reagan. Standard speech; nothing new. Some television reporters do live spots at approximately 10:00 while speeches are in progress.

11:30: return to hotel. Baggage must be in lobby by 6:00 the next morning prior to flight to California.

This is the kind of schedule a campaign reporter faces almost every day. The traveling campaign press corps—often referred to as "the boys and girls on the bus"—follows candidates for months on end, becoming an integral part of the campaign entourage.

During the final weeks of presidential campaigns, this assemblage numbers in the hundreds. Some reporters spend the entire political season on the road; others make brief forays into this hectic world.

A certain glamour is attached to a national campaign— chartered jets zipping back and forth across the country, motor-cades heralded by police sirens, campaign groupies who ogle the recognizable journalists (especially the television correspondents) as well as the candidates.

These trappings of celebrity, however, don't have much to do with the substance of either politics or journalism. Covering a campaign is often a nightmare of complicated logistics, grueling schedules, and other assorted personal and professional discomforts.

Campaign coverage highlights the mutualism of politicians and press. Politicians know the press is essential to the quest for votes. The news media carry the candidates' messages to the public; without the press, campaigning wouldn't accomplish very much.

On the other hand, news organizations devote significant resources to political coverage, counting on campaigns to generate substantial amounts of news that audiences will find attractive.

This mutual reliance produces a give-and-take process in which each side tries to meet its own goals and is quick to complain if it believes it is being forced by the other to operate at a disadvantage.

Limitations on Campaign Coverage

Journalists face a dilemma when covering a campaign. They are, in theory, the public's representatives, charged with conveying objective reports to their audience. They also, however, are usually at the mercy of the campaign they are covering in terms of scheduling, access to the candidate, and other logistical matters.

Careful, thoughtful reporting is tempered by the exigencies of the moment. A campaign trip that visits eight cities in three states in a single day (and this single day might comprise 18 working hours) is likely to leave little time for the journalist to reflect on what he is seeing. Meeting a deadline and finding a way to file a story become the most important tasks; the niceties of analytical reporting take a back seat to more mundane matters.

When a campaign staff member plans the day's events, he is fully aware of the press' deadlines and other time requirements, such as the length of time it will take a courier to carry videotape from the site of a campaign event to a microwave transmission facility. Campaign officials can accommodate the press' needs or ignore them; the decision usually is based on whether their candidate will benefit or be hurt by coverage of a particular event.

For example, if your candidate must make a speech to an audience that might be hostile and you, as one of the campaign managers, want to limit the public's view of this speech (which means limiting the reporting of the speech), you schedule the appearance late in the day—past most press deadlines—or so close to a deadline that news reports will be brief.

By the next day, this will be old news and more current (and less controversial) matters will have to be covered. Scheduling something close to deadline is sometimes called a "squeeze play" because it forces most of the press to battle time problems while trying to report the story.

Even if no ulterior motives dictate this kind of scheduling, time pressure is the reporter's constant nemesis. "News" is often defined by the press as not just what is happening, but what is happening that can be reported in a coherent, timely manner. Some stories never reach a news audience, not because they are not newsworthy, but because they occur at a time or in a place that makes reporting them either impossible or more trouble than they are worth. This doesn't happen to truly important stories; reporters usually find ways to report these even if delays can't be avoided.

The lesson in this is that press "independence" can be illusory. The simple, but at times insurmountable, problem of not having a telephone over which to file a story can affect a day's coverage just as much as an an editor's decision about what events he will assign reporters to.

Campaign coverage is planned around the candidate's schedule, not vice versa; reporters have to figure out how to integrate the demands of the schedule with their own deadline requirements. Most lacking when a reporter's day is governed by such a schedule is the time to do anything more than present a one-dimensional picture of what he has seen. Again, analysis, investigative work, and background research are all likely to be sacrificed to the frantic pace of the day's events.

From the reporter's standpoint, the press and the public are at the mercy of the politicians. The pace the candidate sets is designed not just to win votes but also to control news coverage. By forcing reporters to conform to a carefully shaped schedule, the campaign staff can ensure that the events it considers most important become those most heavily reported.

That means the "good video" of candidate Reagan floating down the San Antonio River is likely to be seen on television newscasts not necessarily because it is the most newsworthy, but because it is the most attractive selection of the day's carefully controlled diet of "media events" fed to the press corps.

Compounding the press' difficulties in finding news amidst propaganda is the organizational structure of many campaigns. The combined mission of campaign staff members is to show off the candidate in the most appealing way and also to protect the candidate from any damage that might be inflicted by the press or the opposition (and, in many cases, to guard against the self-inflicted wounds a candidate's own misstep could cause).

Such protectiveness creates barriers between press and candidate. Campaign planners become so intent on controlling every visible move by their candidate that they instinctively avoid any occasion that might include moments of spontaneity.

Many political strategists are particularly wary about their candidates' contacts with the press, believing them to be inherently dangerous. An off-the-cuff comment or an embarrassing slip of the tongue could cost countless votes. So reporters often run into a wall of silence when seeking comments or other information not only from a candidate but also from senior campaign staff members. Reporters hate to have to include in their stories a line such as, "The candidate was not available for comment." Editors might interpret this as meaning the reporter lacked either the energy or the contacts needed to reach the candidate.

When combined with the rigors imposed by the campaign schedule, these constraints on news gathering can make the reporter's job extremely difficult and can sharpen the adversary nature of relations between press and pols.

Coverage Style: Reporting the "Inside Story"

Reporters' interest in "inside" information has grown as political reporting has focused increasingly not only on what a candidate said or did but *why* something was said or done. With increasing frequency, you see stories about how campaigns are run—who the behind-the-scenes operatives are and what strategies are reflected in the candidate's actions.

This kind of reporting has been in vogue since 1961, when Theodore H. White's *The Making of the President 1960* was published. Considered a breakthrough in political journalism, White's book (which won fame, fortune, and the Pulitzer Prize for its author) detailed the ascent of John Kennedy, taking readers into the proverbial "smoke-filled rooms" where campaign strategy was plotted.

For example, it was White who first analyzed the work of the "Irish mafia," the political team that guided Kennedy's campaign. This book (and successive volumes written about the 1964, 1968, and 1972 campaigns) gave readers a look not only at public matters such as speeches and vote totals, but also at the hitherto unseen machinations of professional politicians—how survey research was interpreted, how television was utilized, and how issues (such as Kennedy's Catholicism) were addressed.

The popularity of White's book gave rise to what is sometimes referred to as the "Teddy White syndrome"—a concentration on reporting about the nuts-and-bolts aspects of campaigning.

This kind of reporting is fine as long as it doesn't overwhelm coverage of the larger issues. Reporters can become such political junkies themselves that they end up doing stories about obscure campaign techniques that are likely to interest only fellow aficionados.

A proper balance should be struck so the public can examine the inner workings of a campaign without losing sight of the issues debate that should be the principal purpose of the campaign. The story of how a candidate prepared for a television debate is interesting, but this should not be covered at the expense of reporting the candidate's views about arms control. It is possible to report both stories.

News organizations shape their coverage partly according to what they think the public is most interested in. When White's "1960" book first appeared and quickly became a bestseller, print and electronic news executives picked up the scent of profits and responded to the public's newly demonstrated desire for White's type of "insider" reporting.

Expectations and Predictions

Digging into campaigners' strategizing has given rise to a new kind of gamesmanship in politics. Reporters try to learn what a campaign staff is planning and then try to evaluate the likely success or failure of those plans and predict how the plans will affect voters. Politicians, on the other hand, know the press is doing this and try to lead reporters to specific topics or interpretations of campaign activity that will benefit the campaign.

This tug-of-war over the news has become an integral aspect of campaigning. Press predictions do much to set public expectations of a candidate's performance.

The all-important rule for the candidate is this: Never let the press set expectations so high that you can't meet them. For example, if you believe you will receive 60 percent of the vote in an upcoming primary, your campaign staff should try to convince the press that you will be lucky to get 50 percent.

That way, if you reach 60 percent, the press is likely to report that you have "exceeded expectations" in the race. If, on the other hand, you tell of your projection of 60 percent and then you receive only 57 percent, you will have "fallen short of the expected vote" and look like a loser even if you receive far more votes than your opponent.

The classic example of this kind of "failure" occurred in 1972 in New Hampshire's important Democratic presidential primary.

Maine Senator Edmund Muskie was considered the odds-on favorite to win his party's nomination. In New Hampshire, neighbor to his home state, Muskie was expected to trounce all his rivals and tighten his grip on the Democratic prize.

The press dutifully gave Muskie the attention due a frontrunner. Muskie's staff responded to this press coverage with what seemed to be acceptable candor but turned out to be disastrous politics: the Maine senator's backers proclaimed they would sweep away their opponents in New Hampshire and garner a healthy majority of the votes.

The press agreed. Reporters and columnists vied for laurels of sagacity as they predicted a Muskie triumph in New Hampshire and went on to take for granted Muskie's nomination and to speculate about his chances against President Richard Nixon in their apparently inevitable match-up in November.

On primary day, approximately 95,000 New Hampshire Democrats cast their ballots. Muskie received 46 percent of the vote; his nearest rival, South Dakota Senator George McGovern, won 37 percent of the total. Obviously, Muskie won a substantial victory.

Not so. In the strange mathematics of political primaries, not only do candidates run against their competitors on the ballot, but also against standards set for them by the press and thus, in theory, by the public.

Muskie defeated his fellow candidates in the pure arithmetic of vote counting, but he lost when measured against the expectations of his voter appeal. The press, encouraged by overconfident Muskie aides, had predicted a landslide. Muskie delivered a victory, but not a landslide. George McGovern, who supposedly would be not only defeated but crushed, was the loser in the vote count but the victor in exceeding expectations.

Because these expectations are so important, politicians and press vie for the upper hand in determining them. Candidates want to manipulate the arithmetic, keeping expectations low so they can exceed them.

To do so, campaign managers have turned poor-mouthing into an art form. These pols try to convince reporters that only a miracle can deliver them from defeat. Most campaign operatives will moan in this way even if they possess private polls showing their candidate 20 points ahead of the pack. Of course, the politicians must be careful not to overdo their lamentations. If they are too convincingly pessimistic, they might scare off contributors and voters.

The strategic plan is to have no place to go but up. If, however, a candidate is perceived as being the frontrunner, he has no place to go but down.

In the 1984 contest for the Democratic presidential nomination, Senator John Glenn proved to be yet another candidate who fell victim to frontrunner's disease. When the 1984 race began, Glenn was expected to seriously challenge Walter Mondale for the nomination. Glenn's campaign, however, showed no early strength. Failing to live up to expectations, Glenn was tagged as a loser.

Senator Gary Hart, on the other hand, had not been expected by many observers to emerge as a serious challenger to Mondale. When Hart started doing better than expected, his candidacy was taken seriously.

This happened even after the Iowa caucuses. Mondale won these overwhelmingly, but Hart ran second, ahead of Glenn and the rest of the pack. Surprised and always in search of a good underdog story, the press began covering Hart more intensively.

By exceeding initial expectations, Hart attracted the press and voter attention that helped propel him to his upset victory over Mondale in the New Hampshire primary.

Hart had both hoped and expected to do better than be a member of the pack of also-rans. His long-term campaign plan, however, was well served by letting the press consider him a longshot (though not merely a noble but doomed candidate such as Harold Stassen) and later tout him as a hot prospect.

Using either independent polling or careful analysis of the campaign's prospects, reporters try to penetrate the propaganda generated by candidates and set reasonable standards against which the candidates' performances may be measured. The ability to accomplish this often reflects the level of the reporter's expertise.

Few journalists have had experience in campaign work. Few have actually knocked on doors to solicit votes or been involved in setting up a telephone bank or direct mail project for a candidate. Of course, this kind of work is unethical once someone becomes a political reporter. The few with such practical experience (such as NBC's Ken Bode) acquired it before their journalistic days, or during a hiatus in their journalism careers.

The value of such knowledge quickly becomes apparent during

a campaign. For example, assume you're a reporter covering a race for mayor in a city of about a million residents. Two weeks before the election, you ask a candidate's press aide how the campaign is faring. He describes the telephone bank operation, proudly telling you that the previous day 500 calls to voters were completed. He seems much impressed with this, and you put it in your story as an example of how well the campaign is functioning. If you'd had experience in campaigns, you would know that 500 calls in that kind of campaign at that point in the race is disastrously low. So you've been conned and your readers have been misled.

From the politician's standpoint, a naive reporter can be a godsend. Lack of expertise means a diminished ability to pierce the smokescreen of self-serving claims that are offered as gospel by the pols. This is part of the game, and it's hard to fault the campaigner for trying to get away with as much as he can. The responsibility rests with the journalist to call the bluff.

Mid-career reporters can't be expected to take sabbaticals and plunge into campaign work. They can, however, be expected to realize that pols will make efforts to take advantage of gaps in their knowledge. Self-education, through studies of past races and careful evaluation of the mechanics of current campaigns, can ensure a certain parity in politician-press relationships.

Any journalists assigned to particular beats, such as medical reporters, are expected to learn the basics of the topics they cover. Perhaps because the language and techniques of politics aren't as intimidating as those of medicine or other such fields, they tend not to be viewed as serious matters for study. That's a mistake, and coverage can suffer as a result.

This kind of game-playing sharpens the adversarial relationship between press and politicians. Each side has its own goals: the candidate wants to win; the reporter wants to present accurate and interesting stories.

Reporting About Political Institutions

Campaigner and reporter both know that the public likes "horse race" stories about the relative prospects of the candidates. Like horse racing, however, this kind of story can have a hypnotic attraction, becoming the principal focus of campaign reporting at the expense of issues-related stories and other substantive matters the press should be covering.

While on the bus, reporters cover the microcosm of politics—the campaign activities happening at that place at that moment. This isn't covering "politics" in the grand sense of that word. Campaign coverage is more akin to reporting about a fire or a bank robbery.

And yet the process itself is an important part of any year's politics. In 1972, George McGovern won the Democratic nomination largely because he mastered the complicated party reforms—they were enacted after being drafted by a committee McGovern chaired—that drastically changed the delegate selection process. In 1976, Jimmy Carter took advantage of the idiosyncrasies of the Iowa caucus system to launch his drive for the presidency.

McGovern's and Carter's successes surprised most people, including many journalists. But they shouldn't have. These candidates played by the rules and it happened that they understood the rules better than their opponents did. The rules governed the make-up of convention delegations, and so governed the selection of the nominee. These were important stories, but most of the press missed them.

A consistent shortcoming of political journalism is its failure to address these broader topics. Politics is not static; the parties and the electorate constantly evolve, sometimes changing dramatically from one election to the next.

Stories about party reform lack the audience appeal of reports on the latest poll results, but that doesn't mean that party business shouldn't be covered. Television news has a particularly difficult time with stories about the system as opposed to those about people; it is hard to explain a complex, although important, party reform in a 90-second television spot. A campaign rally produces good video, but how do you present a picture of "reform"?

Reporting about governmental institutions features similar shortcomings. Coverage of the White House overwhelms coverage of the rest of the government, even though the other branches and even other parts of the executive branch are conducting much important business.

One reason for this emphasis on the presidency is that the president—one person—is easier to cover than numerous cabinet members, congressmen, or other bureaucrats. The White House furthers this emphasis by facilitating press coverage of the president, employing a large press relations staff and even providing electronically wired trees on the White House grounds for use by television correspondents in their "stand-ups."

Of course, the president is the preeminent American government official, but he doesn't run the country by himself. For example, members of the White House staff, who are elected by no one and who generally are accountable only to the president, wield tremendous power. These men and women, however, are rarely seen by the public even though they truly are part of the presidency.

Even during the 1984 presidential race, when the quality of White House leadership was a major issue, few news reports bothered to address the complex topic of how the White House was being run. Focusing on candidates Reagan and Mondale was easier than introducing the public to a large cast of characters, however powerful these men and women might be.

A relationship exists between coverage of governmental or party institutions and the personalities who by choice or circumstance are seen by the public as personifications of those institutions.

For example, in the mid-1970s when the Democratic Party was trying to recover from the Nixon landslide of 1972, coverage of the party was stimulated by the fact that the party's chairman, Robert Strauss, made himself readily available to the press and was "a good interview," always providing reporters with quips that could enliven news reports.

In a similar case, in early 1985, Kansas Senator Robert Dole became a focal point for congressional coverage. As Senate majority leader, Dole could exercise considerable control over President Reagan's economic program and had almost daily comments on the latest efforts to balance the budget and devise tax reforms.

Strauss and Dole stimulated coverage of their respective political institutions by personifying those institutions. "The Democratic Party" and "the Senate" are amorphous without someone to personify them in much the same way in which the president *is* the White House. Persons, not institutions, attract news coverage.

This need for a face is particularly important in television news. The television audience is looking at pictures; something has to be on the screen at every moment. This need for pictures sometimes overwhelms the need to cover important but difficult-to-visualize stories.

In campaign coverage, many reporters shy away from "heavy" issues unless a personality or event exists as a hook to which the story can be attached. This reluctance to address substantive but difficult-to-cover issues perpetuates the tendency of campaign reporting to concentrate on the superficial aspects of politics.

Tensions on the Bus: Print versus Electronic

Meeting the different demands of print and electronic news media is a major responsibility for candidates' press aides. Because of television's impact on voters, television reporters' needs most often are met even if doing so hampers print correspondents' reporting.

Such different needs and different treatment can create tensions within the campaign press corps. Some arrangements are generally accepted; for example, on the press buses television crew members carrying heavy equipment always are given the front rows of seats so they don't have to navigate the aisle and so they can disembark quickly with their gear.

But every so often, print reporters stage a mini-mutiny. They demand that television photographers not be allowed to form a wall between print correspondents and a candidate who is holding a news conference, or they complain that an event providing good video for a television report is not substantive enough to be the basis of a print story.

These complaints are directed partly at the campaign staff but also at colleagues. Relations between print and electronic journalists sometimes are less than cordial. Some print reporters scoff at television news "stars" who, according to the print people, know more about how to blow-dry their hair than about reporting.

Aggravating the rivalry is money. Often a significant difference in salaries exists; a relatively inexperienced television reporter might make several times the pay of a veteran newspaperperson.

In response to print reporters' charges of favoritism benefiting television coverage, campaign staff aides try to calm everyone and push the cameras back. But soon photographers start elbowing their way forward and the television-oriented status quo returns.

Despite the relative youth of the television news business, politicians know how heavily the public relies on "the tube" as a principal source of information about politics and almost everything else. Responsiveness to television's needs, therefore, will be foremost in campaigners' minds even if it bothers the print media's reporters.

Press-Politician Relations

Whatever bickering goes on between print and electronic journalists, common cause is reestablished quickly when the issue is one of ensuring access to a candidate. An "us against them" attitude prevails in press-politician relations, especially during the heat of a campaign.

The intricacies of this adversarial relationship are especially evident at news conferences. Whether on a makeshift platform in the midst of a busy campaign day or in the East Room of the White House before a national television audience, the press conference is not just a test of a politician's skill at using the media for his own purposes; it is also a test of who is the stronger party—press or politician—in the continuing struggle to control the flow of information.

In theory, the news conference is a forum created for the press' benefit. The principal—whether president of the United States or a candidate for city council—makes himself available to the press for questioning.

In most ways, this process hasn't changed much since the first time a politician answered a reporter's question: the reporter is trying to elicit information he wants to know and the politician tries to shape his answer to best serve his own interests. But once again, television has made its impact felt, dramatically changing the procedure and role of the press conference.

This is best seen in the presidential news conference. Television opens the session to millions of Americans, providing an infrequent opportunity to see the president at work. The president responds by making these observers, rather than the assembled press corps, the audience to which he plays.

A news conference that is televised live is an irresistible political tool. A president's standing in the opinion polls usually rises after a televised press conference, a fact not lost on presidents, particularly those seeking reelection. In 1976, for example, President Gerald Ford became much more fond of news conferences during the last days of his campaign against Jimmy Carter.

By claiming he will address some pressing national issue at his news conference, a president usually can convince the television networks to give him free exposure by televising the conference. This "non-political" appearance usually turns out to be more an exercise in vote-seeking than in information dissemination.

In this instance, television allows the politician to go over the heads of news gatherers and directly address the public. The press' role as intermediary vanishes; reporters can become mere props at a news conference. This is particularly likely to happen if the politician holding the conference is adept at sidestepping difficult questions and shaping his answers to meet what he thinks are the interests of his larger audience.

A formalized method by which a president can provide information to the public via the news media is essential to the democratic process. If the president is loathe to establish this linkage, or if journalists aren't diligent in making it work, a dangerous information vacuum can result. The Reagan presidency offers some examples of how this system can fall into disrepair.

One of the lingering images of Ronald Reagan probably will be of him walking across the White House lawn, cupping his hand to his ear as reporters shout questions at him, and then responding with his own shouted answer. The dominating sound will be the loud whine of a helicopter turbine.

This was a neat bit of stageplay by Reagan. He could look affable—a nice guy trying to hear the reporters—while providing virtually no information, and simultaneously scoring some points with the public vis a vis the press by forcing the reporters to appear rude in their shouting.

At one point in 1987, one of these sessions on the lawn brought protests from a group of schoolteachers gathered at the White House for some event of no great consequence. They berated the journalists who, as soon as they spotted the president, started barraging him with questions. When the teachers chastised the reporters, one network correspondent answered, with considerable exasperation, "We're only trying to do our job."

He was correct. The shouting was a product not of inherent press rudeness, but of Reagan's self-imposed isolation. He knew he could minimize his direct, daily accountability to the public if he minimized his contact with the public's surrogates, the White House press corps. Deprived of more reasonable ways to query the chief executive, the reporters were forced to resort to shouting questions whenever the President passed within earshot.

When the stock market crashed in October, 1987, the magnitude of the event was underscored by the White House staff's arranging for Reagan to stop at a microphone on the lawn and comment about the situation. He actually stood still and was close enough so questions didn't have to be shouted.

After that, the President even agreed to a formal, prime time, televised news conference, only his third of the year. Twenty years before, President Lyndon Johnson had held a news conference on the average of once every two weeks. By late 1987, Reagan's average had slumped to one such session every two months.

Most politicians' reluctance to joust with reporters is understandable. Control—that most desired element of anything a pol does—is limited, replaced by dreaded spontaneity. The teleprompter isn't running, the questions aren't known in advance (although most can be anticipated without too much imagination), and the chance of committing a gaffe is substantial.

Some presidents, such as John Kennedy, enjoyed sparring with reporters. Kennedy was fast enough on his feet to be able to dodge when he had to and score his points frequently. If things got rough, he could turn aside a question with a joke. He seemed to enjoy the intellectual gamesmanship of the sessions.

Most presidents aren't that adroit, but some basic rules can be observed to make these events politically rewarding (or at least not damaging) for the president. To do well in news conferences a president requires the following:

• A sense of what is likely to be asked and well-prepared answers to those questions. Most presidents block out several hours of their day when they are holding a news conference in order to rehearse. Staff members ask likely questions and suggest the best ways to answer.

• A realization that sometimes "bland is beautiful." If a question seems to demand an answer that requires more commitment than the president cares to make—on topics such as negotiations with another nation—it's best to keep the answer fuzzy. The truly skilled pol can duck any question, regardless of the interrogator's persistence.

• An understanding of the imagery of the White House. For example, President Reagan's striding down a red-carpet-lined corridor to the podium at his news conferences was a little touch to remind the television audience just who this is and to create a sense of a regal figure granting an audience to the reporters. Those terms might sound offensive, but such subtle maneuvers provide an almost subliminal boost to the president. Flags and other White House trappings also help keep the field of play slightly uneven.

• An appreciation of who the real audience is. The reporters push and tug, but the president need not even bother to brush them aside. He is being judged by the far larger constituency that he reaches through the cameras. If he can look sincere and in command on television, the president suffers little damage even if the reporters aren't satisfied with his answers. Of course, news stories might be done about the quality of his performance, but the live audience—not the day-after analysis—is what matters most.

Most of the tricks of the news conference trade work to the advantage of the president. Though reporters are allowed to ask follow-up questions, the president can usually maintain a modicum of control, suffering only when he is ill-prepared.

Nevertheless, such sessions are far better than nothing. They are visible, relatively spontaneous mechanisms for forcing some presidential accountability.

Given the unwieldy logistics produced by the large size of the White House press corps, some additional forms of give-and-take could be tried, such as more informal briefings for smaller assemblies of reporters, and background sessions to familiarize journalists with the president's thinking without having to deal with the pressures of a nationally broadcast event.

Away from the splendor of the White House, the press-politician relationship becomes more balanced. In the midst of the controlled chaos of the campaign trail, reporters and pols aggressively pursue their respective goals. The journalists try to gather information, the politicians try to shape the news.

This process tends to become a struggle for control over the flow of information. Reporters can gather plenty of newsworthy material on their own, but they also need some cooperation from the candidates and staff members. Any major campaign will offer a rich diet of media events, but real news is often in short supply.

Just as White House correspondents complain about lack of access to the president, so too do campaign reporters protest being relegated to the role of outside spectators at the candidate's carefully staged shows. To do their job properly, journalists must be able to let the public know things about the candidate—experience, temperament, issues positions, electoral prospects—that aren't always discernible in the tightly packaged daily fare of campaigning.

This means the candidate and senior staff members must make themselves available to reporters. Daily campaign press relations often appear to be nothing more than chaotic versions of Reagan's White House lawn shouting matches.

Sometimes during the early primaries, when many of the candidates are desperately trying to remain visible, reporters' needs might be acknowledged. In that situation, the politician depends on the press more than the press on the politician. Candidates sometimes even appear unexpectedly in hotel bars where the press corps has congregated, all smiles and willing to shoot the breeze. This is when tension gives way to the necessities of courtship. By making himself available in this way, the candidate thinks he might inspire interest from some reporters. If interest translates into coverage, score one for the candidate.

Some candidates do, in fact, seem to recognize that the news media have legitimate interests that deserve recognition. Such enlightened attitudes, however, tend to be rare and transient phenomena.

As with White House press relations, the campaign process probably would benefit from a more systematic approach to the linkage between newsmakers and news reporters. More frequent news conferences and increased flexibility in daily scheduling to allow reporters more latitude in their news gathering would be helpful.

Tensions between politicians and journalists are unavoidable, but they need not reach the point at which the flow of information to the voters is seriously impaired. Both sides might find that everyone would benefit from a bit of tolerance.

The intense pace of campaigning poses yet another problem for journalists: How is it possible to maintain a properly broad perspective on the campaign while being swept along as part of one candidate's entourage?

Objectivity is easier to aim for than to reach. Even for reporters totally devoid of bias, the insularity of a campaign creates problems. For example, Tim Crouse, in *The Boys on the Bus*, reports that some knowledgeable journalists covering the latter stages of George McGovern's 1972 presidential campaign thought that McGovern had a chance to win. He ended up carrying Massachusetts and the District of Columbia.

How could these reporters have been so wrong? Look at how they spent their days. When covering McGovern, you go to McGovern rallies. Aside from a few hecklers, all you see are people cheering on this man you are reporting about. You hear optimistic prognostications from campaign staff members you've come to like and respect. It all seems very plausible.

But that's not reality. The real world was occupied by some McGovern supporters, some Nixon supporters, and a lot of people who didn't care one way or the other. On the airplanes and buses of the campaign, everyone is a political junky; outside the campaign orbit is a largely non-political universe.

Considerable intellectual discipline is required for a reporter to resist the effects of the campaign environment. Sometimes it's helpful (if scheduling allows) to take a day off and re-enter the real world. Go to a tavern, a shopping mall, a baseball game, or anyplace else that isn't draped in a campaign's red, white, and blue bunting, and just listen to people. You're unlikely to hear speculation about the latest Gallup poll or debate about what a candidate really meant by his comments regarding domestic content legislation.

Such doses of reality might help keep a reporter from falling prey to imperceptions that arise from traveling in the eye of the storm.

5 | On the Bus— The Candidate's Perspective

In 1980, John Anderson ran for president. He began as a contender for the Republican nomination and ended up as an independent candidate, receiving 5.7 million votes in November.

A congressman from Illinois, Anderson had been identified with the Republican Party's moderate wing, which immediately put him at a disadvantage in the GOP's conservative-dominated nomination process. The chances of someone of Anderson's philosophy emerging as the party's nominee were infinitesimal, as Anderson certainly understood.

Realizing that his post-convention role in national politics would have to be established outside the Republican Party, Anderson early in his efforts targeted not those voters most likely to participate in the GOP selection process, but a much broader segment of the electorate. If Anderson was serious about winning the Republican nomination, this was foolish, but if he was looking ahead to an independent candidacy, it made sense.

Anderson became the quintessential media candidate, building a national, rather than solely Republican, following. While Reagan, Bush, and others made their appeals to traditional GOP power blocs, Anderson courted the national news media by doing iconoclastic things (such as speaking in favor of gun control before a staunchly conservative group) that were virtually certain to alienate Republicans but would guarantee receiving news coverage.

Reporters bored by traditional intra-party politicking gravitated to Anderson, and Anderson clung tightly to his friends in the press. He became the darling of columnists who despaired of the intellectual vacuity promised by a Carter-Reagan contest. Anderson's appearance and his ability to craft learned-sounding pronouncements won him, if not votes, at least ample discussion on the op-ed pages and on television.

Despite his virtually non-existent chances of becoming president, Anderson received phenomenal coverage. The reason: He gave reporters what they wanted—a different angle from which to cover a tedious campaign.

In retrospect, Anderson can be viewed as just another ambitious politician who happened to figure out how to use the press to his advantage. Of course, Anderson never came close to achieving his quixotic quest; he captured no electoral votes. But he acquired a national forum for his views and did so with only minimal reliance on traditional party mechanisms. He went to voters via news media, not via party.

History will treat Anderson's effort as a mildly interesting footnote to the Carter-Reagan race, but Anderson's successful cultivation (and perhaps manipulation) of the press offers useful lessons to candidates. Anderson unabashedly made the news media his principal audience and emerged from obscurity by doing so.

Stroking the press is a political art form that in some ways takes precedence over traditional political strategy. The "media candidate" is someone who not only understands the technology of the modern news business, but also can use the media's power as the basis of his campaign plan.

As with other elements of campaigning, press relations requires a carefully planned strategy that can generate helpful news coverage and aid in the quest for votes.

The candidate's strategy can be divided into four basic goals:

1. determining what issues will be covered;
2. projecting a "personality" helpful in wooing voters;
3. ensuring a steady volume of coverage;
4. encouraging a positive tone in the coverage.

If a candidate and his staff can craft a media strategy that will accomplish all these tasks, press coverage will probably prove an important asset.

Picking Issues to Emphasize

Deciding what issues are covered during a campaign does not occur in a vacuum. Reporters, editors, and producers are often guided by the candidates' choice of issues, and only occasionally will the press try to direct the public's attention to issues that the candidates have not previously determined as topics for campaign debate.

Most candidates follow a simple formula for finding their issues. Based on survey research, the politicians decide what issues generate the most public interest and then shape political positions to respond to those interests. In simplest terms, the pol figures out what the voters want to hear and then tells it to them.

Common sense can also help a candidate control what is covered by a particular publication or broadcast station. For example, when campaigning in a rural area, a statewide candidate can talk about farm policy and focus press attention on his views, or he can talk about esoteric aspects of defense policy and find the initiative taken away from him by reporters who want to talk about the farm issues in which their audience is most interested.

The news media, like politicians, have constituencies to which they must remain accountable if they want their circulation or rating points to remain high. Smart politicians know this and anticipate press interests.

This happens even during presidential campaigns. In 1980, for instance, candidate Ronald Reagan was available for one-on-one interviews by local television stations, during which he kept the focus of the interview on issues of local significance, such as how many new jobs his policies would create in that station's viewing area.

An aggressive candidate can usually control the direction of an interview, slipping around questions he doesn't want to answer and pounding home the message he has decided he wants to get across. A candidate's success or failure might be determined by the extent to which the press allows him to control the topics most heavily covered.

Another way candidates influence what is covered is through their control of the campaign schedule. Speeches or releases about topics the candidate wants covered occur at times during the day when members of the press corps are most likely to use the material in their stories. Issues that the candidate feels he must address but would prefer to receive scant coverage can be brought up at times inconvenient to the press.

Of course, reporters can ignore all such efforts at manipulation and focus on whatever issues they think are most important. But in the course of a long campaign, the candidate's emphasis often enough will influence the press' emphasis.

Projecting a Personality

Creating the candidate's public persona is seen by many campaign professionals as their most important task. The charming, charismatic leader who smiles upon the public from billboards and television screens might be a fine person or a consummate jackass; the distinction blurs once the campaign's image makers do their work.

As with most aspects of a campaign, image-building relies heavily on polling data. What the public thinks an officeholder should be usually becomes a self-fulfilling expectation; the candidate will fit whatever mold the public wants filled. Different elected offices and different constituencies demand different kinds of candidates. Statesman, investigator, caretaker—what the voters want the voters usually receive.

Getting press coverage to reflect the chosen image isn't always easy. Campaign staff members undertake much missionary work to convince reporters of the greatness of their candidate.

Ronald Reagan has always fared well in the process. His image as avuncular but tough, folksy but shrewd, might seem so self-contradictory that it would be shredded by the press. But most press coverage of Reagan (at least until the Iran-contra scandal) has bolstered rather than debunked this image.

Similar to selecting the issues, shaping the candidate's image depends largely on controlling the press' relationship with the candidate and the campaign. Striking the proper balance between the open door campaign and the overly sequestered candidate is essential.

The 1972 presidential race saw candidates at both ends of this spectrum. Democratic nominee George McGovern was so intent on being the antithesis to Richard Nixon that he opened his campaign to unrestrained press scrutiny. In principle that is fine, but in practice it meant that neither McGovern nor his staff could enjoy the privacy needed to marshal ideas and energies for their campaign.

The perils of openness became apparent during the Eagleton crisis soon after the Democratic National Convention. Revelations of vice presidential nominee Senator Thomas Eagleton's history of mental illness plunged the McGovern camp into chaos as the candidate and his strategists tried to decide what to do with Eagleton.

Press coverage didn't create the crisis, but it certainly exacerbated the Democrats' problems. The McGovern camp's open door policy let the public see much of the anguish that resulted in McGovern looking alternately scheming or indecisive.

The press was first told that McGovern was "one thousand percent" behind Eagleton. Then McGovern announced Eagleton was resigning his position on the ticket. While this drama was unfolding, the press corps was running wild, feeding on leaks (some accidental and some intentional) from McGovern and his staff.

In retrospect, McGovern undoubtedly would have been better served if he had been able to resolve the Eagleton mess privately, keeping himself and the issue out of the public's eye until he had decided what he was going to do. Unable to shut out the press once the doors had been opened, McGovern looked like a buffoon while he stumbled through his decision-making.

Remaining true to the niceties of candidate-press relations was McGovern's undoing. In theory, the public was well served by being able to see all that was going on, but McGovern's surrendering his privacy was the equivalent of yielding control of his own campaign.

McGovern's problem probably generated amazed delight among Richard Nixon's advisers. Nixon considered himself a brutalized victim of the press, particularly during his unsuccessful campaigns for president in 1960 and for governor of California in 1962.

The bitterness born in these defeats took the form of an undying enmity towards the news media, and this in turn led Nixon to keep as far removed as possible from the press during his victorious presidential races in 1968 and 1972.

Nixon's theory seemed to be that no good could come from letting the press get too close to the candidate or to the inner workings of the campaign. Whenever possible (which turned out to be most of the time), the Nixon campaign communicated with the press from a carefully calculated distance, relying on news releases rather than news conferences and eliminating every possible element of spontaneity from the campaign.

In terms of communicating a candidate's image to the public, these different strategies produced different kinds of pictures of the candidates. McGovern's portrait was truly drawn from life, accurate to the point of illustrating his flaws. Nixon's portrayal by the press, however, was more a result of distant glimpses that produced a less realistic but also less controversial image.

The lesson for politicians in this 1972 story is that "bland is beautiful." A skillfully created image is likely to prove more politically beneficial than is a completely honest depiction of a candidate.

However far open a candidate decides the door to his campaign will be, the staff members responsible for press liaison are constantly trying to put a favorable "spin" on reporters' impressions of their candidate. Campaign professionals know (based on their polling) what kind of candidate the voters want to see, so these pols do whatever they can to make certain the news media deliver this image to the public.

Volume of Coverage

Not only must a favorable image of the candidate be created, but this image must reach the public continuously. Candidates don't just want good coverage; they want *lots* of good coverage.

To stimulate a steady volume of coverage, campaign planners schedule an unending stream of "media events" designed to feed the press' insatiable appetite for pretty pictures, candidate speeches that can be summarized in a few words, and easily described activity. (Handshaking to the accompaniment of brass bands and cheerleaders is always a favorite.)

Media events are the trademark of the modern campaign that seeks to reach the voters not directly, but solely via the news media.

Particularly during presidential campaigns, with their heavy emphasis on security, many of these events take place outside the view of the general public. Whatever audience is allowed to be present is usually there only for its value as background for news photos.

The perfect media event is short, simple, scheduled not too close to deadline, and above all, in the television age, "visual."

For example, if a candidate wants to give a speech about defense policy, he could give it in an auditorium where press and audience could simply hear what he has to say. But this candidate's chances of getting television time would be greatly enhanced if he would deliver his speech at a military base, with tanks or jets in the background, and with the opportunity to make a perfunctory inspection of the base, giving the photographers some useful "cover video" to fill any gaps in a television story.

Media events don't happen by accident. One of the most important jobs in a campaign is that of the "advance person," the staff member who reaches a place well ahead of a politician's arrival and makes whatever arrangements are necessary to ensure that the pol will be seen in the best possible light.

During the first Reagan term, White House aide Michael Deaver scored legendary triumphs in his staging of presidential appearances. For example, President Reagan's June, 1984, visit to Normandy on the fortieth anniversary of D Day not only secured moving news coverage but also (and not coincidentally) provided video for effective campaign propaganda later in the year.

Some media events have become so common that they are political cliches. For example, any candidate campaigning in Texas will find time to visit San Antonio and deliver a speech (preferably filled with hard-line defense rhetoric) in front of the Alamo. Cliche or not, the visual aspect of such an appearance is irresistible to most television producers and is likely to ensure some air time for the candidate.

The goal for a campaigner is not merely to create a good event occasionally, but to plan one every day. Particularly on slow days when the candidate is neither saying nor doing anything exceptional, the cleverly staged media event can be the day's salvation, garnering some coverage through gimmickry if nothing else.

Voters' attention spans are notoriously short. Candidates need to remain in the public eye or they will be forgotten. As discussed in

Chapter One, receiving no coverage can be worse than receiving negative coverage.

Late-starting candidates are damaged at the outset because they, too, will often have a difficult time convincing the press to cover them. This again highlights a classic "Catch 22" of politics: you can't win without press coverage, but you won't get press coverage unless you prove you can win.

In 1987, Missouri Congressman Richard Gephardt, running for the Democratic presidential nomination, showed he understood this principle. He made trade protectionism his main issue when the United States and Japan were engaged in intricate maneuvering to avoid a full-blown trade war. By sponsoring trade legislation at this time and speaking to this issue daily, Gephardt was covered regularly (as he knew he would be). This helped him establish an identity as being more than just "one of the pack" of candidates, at least until this issue lost its luster.

Tone of Coverage

Voters' opinions are shaped not only by the amounts of news coverage of persons and issues, but also by the tone of that coverage.

The tone of coverage can be affected by a variety of tactics a campaign might launch. A candidate's aide might make suggestions for feature or sidebar stories that would show the politician in a favorable light (for example, a story about a congressional candidate who is a Vietnam veteran visiting former comrades in Veterans' Administration hospitals).

Similarly, every effort is made by campaign staff members to prevent unflattering stories about their candidate. In 1976, President Gerald Ford's campaign was plagued by stories about his clumsiness, physical and verbal. None of the stories explicitly attacked Ford's ability to govern, but they portrayed him as something of a buffoon, thus undermining the respect this unique, unelected president needed if he was to win.

Politicians sometimes anticipate stories that could inject a negative tone into coverage and take preemptive measures to neutralize such matters. In 1980, for example, Ronald Reagan's advisers were worried about "the actor issue": Would voters have qualms about putting a former actor in the White House?

Rather than trying to dodge the issue, Reagan met it head-on, saying he was proud of his work in Hollywood, where he had led an actors' guild and had learned to work with many kinds of people. The forthrightness and humor with which Reagan discussed his acting career seemed to settle the matter; it never became a significant factor in the campaign.

Successful candidates rarely just await press coverage. Instead, they not only aggressively seek coverage per se, but also try to affect the substance and tone of that coverage. A candidate who is too passive surrenders much of the control he might exercise over how voters shape their opinions.

When the tone of news coverage of a certain candidate is respectful, the public pays attention and that candidate's campaign develops the mysterious force known as "momentum."

Momentum is as much discussed by political journalists as it is by sportscasters. The same intangible quality invoked as a football team marches down a gridiron—its mysterious power defying definition—is as reverently discussed in politics as in sports.

In politics, momentum can have a noticeable effect on various aspects of a campaign. Evidence (in polls or early voting) that a candidate has a chance of winning is likely to attract news coverage. As that coverage raises the candidate's profile, more coverage takes place. Campaign momentum and the news coverage it generates are self-perpetuating. Winning generates coverage, which in turn improves chances for continuing to win.

The George Bush presidential campaign of 1980 provides a good example. Starting early, Bush upset Ronald Reagan in January's Iowa caucuses. Bush had captured, as he put it, "big mo" and used this momentum to overshadow other challengers.

The appearance of momentum and the attention it attracts also help a candidate's fund raising. Bush in 1980 and Gary Hart in 1984 are examples of candidates who were able to go to contributors, display their pictures on the cover of *Newsweek*, and say: "Look, the press says this campaign is rolling. We have momentum and so we're a good investment for your campaign dollars."

Most campaign contributors temper their idealism with realism. They like to back winners, not noble also-rans. Evidence of momentum—success and a prognosis for further victories—can loosen pursestrings. To cite 1984 again, Hart's apparent momentum probably pulled some contributions away from Alan Cranston and the other Democratic candidates trying to derail Walter Mondale.

Voting, too, is influenced by momentum and the attraction of supporting a likely winner. Like the campaign contributor, the voter evaluates the credibility of a candidacy's prospects.

Defining what actually constitutes momentum is difficult, but candidates know that whatever it is, they want it and they know that the news media can help give it to them.

This results in a ritualistic process in which candidates proclaim (to the public, but principally to the press) that their campaigns possess this magical ingredient. Frequent lobbying of reporters is undertaken by campaign staffers whose mission is to have their candidate identified in news stories as the principal possessor of momentum. Underlying these efforts is the assumption that reporters, contributors, and voters will gravitate to the momentum-wielding candidate.

These efforts must be handled gingerly by the candidate's aides. Overselling the notion of momentum can create a dangerous trap: expectations for the candidate might reach perilous heights. So the ultimate goal is to portray the candidate as making progress but not having reached the point at which he becomes a target for other candidates' potshots.

All this might seem rather silly: maneuvering and speculation about a characteristic no one can even define very well. But political prowess is at least partly illusory, and momentum—real or imagined—will continue to be claimed by candidates.

"Care and Feeding" of the Press

Particularly in presidential campaigns, when press coverage is intensive but the candidate himself is only infrequently available to the press, the staff is the crucial link between campaign and press, and thus between candidate and public.

Aides, not candidates, answer most questions about issues positions, schedules, and other items of daily campaign business. When you read a reporter's assertion such as, "The response of the Mondale campaign to Reagan's comment was that the President doesn't understand the issue," you may assume that the reporter talked to an aide, not to the candidate himself, to get the information.

The press corps is quick to judge a candidate's competence based on what the reporters think of staff members' abilities. Proper care and feeding of the press beast is an important staff function. Reporters who distrust or have no respect for staff members are likely to shape similarly negative opinions about the candidate. As a rule, the most successful candidates are those with the best staffs.

Efforts to influence the tone of coverage are part of the continuing courtship of news persons by politicians. This wooing is born of necessity; feelings between press and pols usually range from mistrust to loathing, with only an occasional sprinkling of affection.

Regardless of feelings, the care and feeding of the press can be neglected only at a candidate's peril. After all, reporters are human and are subject to constant personal and professional pressures during a long campaign. Inevitably, schedules will collapse, meals will be missed, luggage will be lost, and headaches will be epidemic.

Despite such problems, the reporters will be turning out stories. Most politicians have sense enough to know that a hungry, tired, sullen reporter is unlikely to have anything nice to say about anyone, especially the candidate being covered.

A campaign staff's response to press needs can have at least a subconscious effect on reporters' perceptions of the campaign. A staff implicitly conducts a kind of psychological warfare on behalf of its candidate. A helpful staff is seen by reporters as the mark of a competent candidate. Uncooperative campaign personnel, on the other hand, exacerbate tensions between press and politicians.

Lobbying by campaign staff members attracted considerable attention during the 1984 presidential campaign with the advent of "spin squads" deployed after the Reagan-Mondale debates. These teams of campaign personnel descended on reporters covering the debates and presented their reasons for believing that their candidate had bested his opponent.

Reporters didn't seem to pay much attention to this campaign within the campaign, but the effort was noteworthy because it was so blatant and became itself the subject of news stories.

Campaigners defend this kind of press-directed pressure as essential public relations. The controlling theory for a candidate seems to be, "If I don't say nice things about myself, no one else is going to do it for me." That logic dictates a two-pronged campaign, directed at the public directly and via the news media.

Although a candidate might neither like nor respect the reporters covering his campaign, every sensible politician recognizes the importance of the news media in shaping voting behavior. Candidates try, with various degrees of subtlety, to influence how the press does its job, and no candidate would be so foolish as to disregard the reporters covering his campaign.

Most journalists remain neutral (at least in the sense of keeping overt bias out of their reporting) and some are friendly, producing stories that, in the candidate's judgment, benefit his cause. But some reporters may be implacably hostile, either overtly so or judged so because of the tone of their stories. This latter category usually isn't very large, but it is troublesome for the campaign manager and press secretary. Can the impact of such reporters be minimized?

Yes, but it must be done with extreme care. This is an instance in which high-sounding principles and ethics take a back seat to political reality. From the candidate's standpoint, negative news coverage constitutes a hostile act. It can't simply be shrugged off with the comment, "Oh, well; the First Amendment is wonderful. Our journalist friend is entitled to his opinion." The damage that might be done—especially if the reporter in question represents a television network or a major newspaper or magazine—is too great to allow such kindly philosophizing.

From the campaign manager's or press secretary's view, the question isn't whether to respond, but how to do so. The worst thing to do is to publicly attack the reporter. Even if his colleagues don't like him, and even if they think his coverage has been unfair, they are likely to circle the wagons and help defend one of their own. So instead of having just one angry reporter, the entire press corps might end up being antagonized.

Subtle tactics are more effective. Does the reporter want a one-on-one interview with the candidate? "Fine, your request will be carefully considered." Sure. The request will be carefully considered when hell freezes over. Until then, bureaucratic inertia takes over. Does the reporter want to participate in one of the campaign manager's background sessions about the progress of the campaign?

"We're sorry you missed the one last night. We must have forgotten to tell you about it. We'll put you on the list for the next one. No, we're not certain when that will be." Does the reporter want to know why advance word about an important speech the candidate plans to give was leaked to other reporters but not to him? "We don't know how that information leaked. Sorry, we can't help you about that."

The reporter can scream about being discriminated against, but he'll be hard-pressed to make much of a case. Also, because no overt action has been taken against him that might be judged as a slap at the press corps as a whole, his colleagues are unlikely to be sympathetic. After all, they're gaining a slight competitive edge by virtue of another reporter being left out of part of the information loop.

This isn't quite as Machiavellian as it might sound, but it provides an idea of the hard-ball realities of the campaign game. News coverage can help a lot or it can hurt a lot. The politicians respond in ways appropriate to protecting their interests.

Such confrontation is best avoided altogether. Sometimes the press versus pol conflicts arise because of misjudgments of one side about the other. If a candidate or member of his campaign staff thinks a reporter can be swayed through enticements such as exclusive interviews or leaks, a big mistake is being made. Most journalists—and certainly all the good ones—can't be bought that way, and they can't be alienated by slights from the politician. They just do their job of gathering and reporting the news.

Politicians sometimes get a nasty surprise when they misjudge a journalist's loyalties. For example, in 1972, some members of George McGovern's campaign staff were so certain that reporters liked their candidate's openness and honesty and disliked Richard Nixon's anti-press attitude that they expected a deluge of favorable coverage.

They didn't get it. Reporters covering McGovern did appreciate the Democratic nominee's relative candor, but this didn't mean that stories about the campaign would be slanted in his favor. Many members of McGovern's staff grew increasingly bitter about what they thought was a betrayal by their "friends" in the press corps. That attitude is evidence of badly misreading journalists' sense of duty.

Similar problems arose during Edward Kennedy's race against Jimmy Carter for the Democratic presidential nomination in 1980. Kennedy's supporters expected to benefit from longstanding relationships with reporters dating back to John Kennedy's campaign in 1960 and Robert Kennedy's candidacy in 1968. Knowing that journalists weren't particularly friendly towards Carter, some members of Kennedy's staff had counted on positive news coverage as a major tool in their efforts to wrest the nomination away from the president.

Again, it didn't happen. Reporters covered Kennedy just as rigorously as they would have treated anyone else. In fact, the Kennedy camp's assumptions may have backfired. Journalists knew that politicians and public alike were expecting a press tilt towards Kennedy, so some reporters may have overcompensated, treating Kennedy more harshly than necessary just to prove absence of bias.

When this happens, the whole system is thrown out of whack. Reporters shouldn't have to compensate or overcompensate for perceptions of possible favoritism. All such matters get in the way of straightforward reporting of the news.

As Americans rely ever more heavily on news sources for political information, the campaigner finds his electoral fortunes increasingly at the mercy of how he is covered. Volume and tone of coverage can be more important than the substance of the campaign. Reporters' opinions about the candidates' abilities are likely to influence thousands of voters' opinions and thus can affect election outcomes.

Politicians must keep this whole process in proper perspective. Sometimes they become victims of their own distorted outlook about the role of the press. They think—wishfully or fearfully—that news coverage by itself will make or break their campaign.

True, the news media are crucial in conveying information to the public, but the press in only a vehicle. When the politician becomes overly intent on trying to manipulate news coverage—whether through courtship or bullying—the balance of power is threatened.

This problem is rooted in a misunderstanding—or at least a forgetfulness—concerning the respective roles of politician and journalist.

6 | Finding Room for Ethics

Protected by a vague mandate granted by the First Amendment, the American press finds itself with extensive power and very few restraints on that power. Responsibility must be self-imposed; ethical standards must be self-determined.

The news media control the flow of political information to voters and thus play a crucial role in determining electoral outcomes and shaping public attitudes about policy. This exercise of power demands a commensurate exercise of responsibility. The basic job of the press is to *inform*, not to make voters' decisions for them and not to serve as a propaganda channel for politicians.

How Competent Are Political Journalists?

An overriding ethical issue is that of basic competence. Do political journalists know enough about politics to cover the field properly?

In all too many cases, the answer is no. Reporters unfamiliar with the mechanics of campaigns, the complexities of issues, and even the structure of the political system often are victimized by pols who know the journalists' business better than the journalists know politics.

The old adage that "knowledge is power" is true. On a practical level, a journalist's knowledge of politics can be a stabilizing force, helping to keep candidates and officials honest and raising the level of political debate.

Considerable political expertise is essential as reporters and their news organizations make one of their most important decisions: Who among the candidates should be covered most extensively?

The impact of the "screening process" is obvious. Candidates recognize the correlation between the volume of news coverage and the extent of voter consideration of their candidacies.

This is a classic example of press power that must be tempered by press responsibility. News organizations have to decide who gets how much coverage. Perfect even-handedness is impossible, but carefully developed criteria (using polling data and varied analyses of candidates' prospects) should be the basis for making coverage decisions.

The press predisposition should be to cover more candidates rather than fewer, even if just for the sake of letting the voters see how inept some of the politicians are.

Journalists, however, sometimes adopt a rather cavalier attitude towards their de facto screening role. Reporters might not understand (or if they understand, they ignore) how much influence they exert.

This ethical blind spot—whether it is the product of ignorance or laziness—undermines press credibility and provides ample fuel for critics who charge that the press is to politics what the bull is to the china shop.

Investigative Reporting

Press power makes itself felt in many ways besides the screening process. Politics always has been fertile ground for investigative reporters. The renowned heroics of Woodward and Bernstein in the Watergate case have spurred the ambitions of countless other reporters who dream of Pulitzer Prizes, lavish book contracts, and other fringe benefits of fame.

Even the most noble intentions, however, must exist within an ethical framework. The slashing style of those investigative reporters who shoot first and seek the facts later can do tremendous damage that lingers long after the headlines have disappeared.

The public is also sensitive to what it sees as persecution by the press. Even politicians—never held in high public esteem—receive public sympathy if it seems they are being hounded mercilessly by reporters.

When does investigative journalism stop being reporting and become harassment? No clear line exists between the two, but the public instinctively seems to sense when the press has gone too far.

Sometimes reporting requires persistence even in the face of public opinion. In the early days of Watergate, for example, many people believed that Richard Nixon was merely the victim of a press vendetta. Finally, after all the news reports, the congressional investigations, and Nixon's resignation, public opinion had shifted and the diligent journalists who pursued the story received the applause they deserved. Much the same thing happened as the Reagan administration's Iran-contra scandal unfolded.

Of course, stories don't always turn out with the politician proving to be as guilty of grievous sins as the press first alleges.

A good example of press zealousness (and perhaps over-zealousness) was seen during the 1984 presidential campaign when Democratic vice presidential nominee Geraldine Ferraro was the subject of countless news stories regarding allegedly improper financial activities.

Day after day, stories appeared accusing Ferraro of filing inaccurate finance reports, accusing her husband of ties to organized crime, and generally portraying the nominee as a woman with much to hide.

At the time, no law enforcement agency seemed to take this very seriously, but the press pursued Ferraro with a vengeance.

The reasons behind this spectacle of "investigative journalism" aren't clear. Geraldine Ferraro isn't Richard Nixon; no long-standing antipathy between the press and Ferraro existed that might explain the fury of the congresswoman's pursuers.

Nor was the alleged wrongdoing something that endangered the republic. The Watergate story dealt with criminal conspiracy in the White House and tampering with the electoral process. In Ferraro's case, few people (and few journalists) ever seemed to understand what she supposedly had done wrong.

The Ferraro story became investigation for the sake of investigation. No prosecutor could have done what the press did without his target demanding warrants and filing a civil suit to block harassment. The press, on the other hand, to a considerable extent writes its own rules. Aside from filing libel suits (an alternative that probably would have been politically and legally unproductive), Ferraro had no recourse.

One of the most vivid scenes of the 1984 campaign was the long press conference Ferraro held to try to explain her finances and put the matter to rest. Reporters battered Ferraro with what often seemed poorly reasoned questions, and Ferraro held her own.

Many people watching the session saw not a slippery politician being unmasked by a vigilant press, but rather a decent officeholder being persecuted while trying to uphold her own and her family's honor.

Potential candidates observing these goings-on probably shuddered at the thought of being subjected to such an inquisition and turned away from politics. That is the kind of residual effect the press' work can have. The ripples from such an "investigation" can reach far.

Inquiries into Ferraro's finances were not wrong; anyone seeking high public office must expect scrutiny from the press and voters. In this case, however, the news media seemed unconscious of the ethical framework within which their power should be exercised.

In 1987, press zealousness again was questioned when *Miami Herald* reporters staked out Democratic frontrunner Gary Hart's Washington home to see if Hart was spending the night with a woman other than his wife. The newspaper then ran a story saying Hart was doing so, and the former senator, who long had been plagued by rumors of infidelity, terminated his candidacy a few days later.

When he dropped out of the race, Hart blasted a system in which he said reporters had become the hunters and candidates the hunted. Casting himself as victim, Hart tried to blame his demise more on press unscrupulousness than on his own poor judgment.

Was Gary Hart treated unfairly? Hart knew (or should have known) that when you run for president you surrender most of your privacy. That is a price you pay to play in the big leagues of politics. And because many people vote for the person—not for party or issues—the standards and behavior of candidates deserve scrutiny. After all, personal moral principles certainly will affect a president's policy-making.

The argument for leaving Hart alone is flawed. Suppose the press had ignored the many allegations about Hart's philandering. And suppose Hart ended up as president. And further suppose that the Hart White House was shaken by a sex scandal. Wouldn't you then be angry if you learned the press had had information about Hart but withheld it?

The reporters staking out Hart's house didn't trespass or entrap or do anything illegal. They asked Hart to comment on what they had found. Earlier, Hart himself had suggested that if reporters were intrigued by his personal life they should follow him. Hart said they would be bored. He was wrong.

Hart not only exercised bad judgment, but he flaunted it. To have ignored his behavior would have been journalistic negligence.

The "Character" Issue

By early 1987, the 1988 presidential campaign was well underway. The federal deficit dangled above the nation's economy like Damocles' sword. Defense spending was poised to make a quantum jump upwards because of the "star wars" Strategic Defense Initiative. Latin American peace plans were stalled. The Persian Gulf war threatened to ensnare more nations. American-Soviet negotiations to curtail the arms race offered encouragement one day and gloom the next.

Any of these matters would seem a logical choice as the principal topic for debate among presidential candidates and the most worthy subject for extensive news coverage. Instead, however, the dominant issue became the "character" of the candidates.

Gary Hart was the first to fall, once his dalliance with model Donna Rice was publicized. Joe Biden succumbed next, after allegations of plagiarism in campaign speeches and misrepresentation about his law school accomplishments. Other candidates were also subjected to pummeling about their morality or judgment.

It's hard to summon much sympathy for someone like Hart, who dared reporters to follow him and flaunted his extra-marital escapades. But it's also difficult to respect journalists who so obviously relish their search for sleazy items normally found in the tabloids available at supermarket check-out counters.

Journalistic priorities can easily become skewed. Rumor and speculation can displace straight reporting and analysis. The quest for insights into personalities can overwhelm serious consideration of issues. For instance, when Biden dropped out of the race, most voters knew more about his law school record than about his record in the Senate.

Character is certainly a legitimate issue in itself. Voters need to know about the persons who aspire to become the world's most powerful popularly elected leader—what motivates them, what their values are, how they are likely to behave under stress. In probing character, however, some concern about relevance must exist. A candidate's opinion about adultery might be interesting, but his thoughts about arms control and tax policy are more crucial.

Also, even a presidential candidate is entitled to some personal privacy. When reporters demand carte blanche right of access to medical histories, financial records, and every other aspect of someone's life, they should be able to explain why this information is necessary. Reporters' idle curiosity shouldn't be reason enough, and if a candidate resists acceding to such demands, that isn't reason enough to assume he's hiding dark secrets.

When reporting becomes inquisition, journalists should back off long enough to engage in some introspection. Such self-examination is essential, especially given the impact of 30 seconds on a network newscast or three paragraphs in a major newspaper. The reach of this exposure is incalculable, especially if that bit of coverage is imbued with a tinge of sensationalism.

The fall of Hart illustrated this reach quite well. Here was a man well on his way to his party's presidential nomination. He had been running hard for four years. But then, after just one week under fire from the news media, he was finished. Regardless of Hart's virtues or lack of them, his demise provides real instruction in the relative powers of press and politicians. Of course, journalists have no obligation to protect inept or blameworthy candidates, but they also have no need to wreak havoc indiscriminately.

Political journalism is still an evolving craft. Squaring aggressive reporting with ethical responsibilities takes much time and thought. This is a task that cannot be neglected; to do so not only risks serious damage to the tenuous balance of trust that exists between news and political professionals, but also jeopardizes the public's faith in the integrity of journalists.

If news consumers decide that scandal rather than substance has come to dominate the news product, their skepticism is likely to increase to the point at which journalists will face a formidable loss of public trust. All those juicy stories aren't worth that.

Leaks and Manipulation

Sometimes the tables are turned and the press is manipulated by politicians. The most common way this happens is through the planned "leak" of information. The reporter might think he has uncovered a hot story, but actually he may unwittingly be doing the politician a favor.

In exchange for information, the person leaking material might request anonymity. The information itself might be gossip about an opponent, premature release of a speech text, or virtually anything else likely to serve the leaker's purposes.

If the journalist plays the game, granting anonymity and using the information, he is, to a certain extent, surrendering his control over his reporting. His audience will attach credibility (based on the reputation of the reporter or his news organization) to the story despite the source not being revealed.

This presents an ethical dilemma journalists often face, whether covering politics or anything else. When are you making a deal with a source that will benefit the public, and when does the deal benefit just the source?

Before providing a politician with unobstructed news access to the public, the reporter should question the source's motives.

For example, if a campaign worker for Candidate A confidentially leaks some information about Candidate B's once having been arrested, how should the reporter proceed? The best course would be to find independent, on-the-record verification of the story. But if, for some reason, this isn't possible and the reporter is convinced the leaked information is accurate and important, he probably should run the story.

But before attributing the story to "a source who spoke on condition that his identity not be revealed," the reporter should ask what purpose is served by cloaking the involvement of Candidate A's supporter.

Shielding the source's identity makes it difficult for the public to decide on the credibility of the story. Knowing that the story originated with Candidate B's opponent might make many readers or viewers skeptical about the information.

Sometimes a source needs to be protected if, for instance, releasing the information jeopardizes the source's job. Also, if the journalist believes the source is reliable and has access to valuable information, he might be worth cultivating. That could involve a promise of anonymity.

The ethical imperative for the journalist is to remember that he is the public's agent. The reporter covering politics has the chance his audience doesn't have to question sources and to decide whether a given item is news or propaganda.

Even without raising the issue of anonymity, politicians often try to manipulate journalists. Reporters encounter everything from straightforward self-promoting to clever misrepresentation. Sometimes it is hard to distinguish between truth and falsity in politics, particularly if the journalist lacks the knowledge and energy to do his job properly.

Attempts to manipulate the press occur almost constantly during campaigns. For example, a campaign staff might release a poll showing broad public support for their candidate. An unwary journalist might take the poll at face value. Polls aren't always what they seem to be. What was the sample size? How was it selected? What were the questions? When was the survey conducted? All these matters can significantly affect the poll's results.

If, for instance, the poll was released by a Republican candidate and it shows him leading his Democratic opponent by a substantial margin, reporters should make certain the sample polled did not contain a disproportionate number of Republicans and that the questions were not "loaded" in a way likely to elicit a favorable response.

Releasing such phony poll results doesn't happen too often, but when it does it clearly is an example of unethical campaigning. For journalists to blithely report those poll results as accurate is at least equally unethical. The motivation is irrelevant. It doesn't matter that the reporter didn't know the poll was rigged. The journalist's responsibility to the public is such that he is obligated to check such matters before he reports to his audience.

The same kind of issue arises when a candidate's staff member tells reporters covering a campaign rally that at least 10,000 persons are in the audience. A reporter who accepts that without testing it against his own judgment and reports it to the public as fact is irresponsible (especially if the crowd total is really only 2,000).

This kind of situation illustrates a fundamental issue of political journalism: How extensive should be the control *politicians* exercise over the political process and the flow of information about that process?

Journalists must think about this because they are the only logical counter-balance to politicians' dominance. As the voters' surrogates, reporters can't afford to be too passive.

But at the same time, the news media are outsiders. After all, the journalists aren't seeking votes, nor are they casting a determinative number of votes. As "reporters" in the truest sense, do journalists have the right to play some role in governing the way the process works?

On a theoretical level, such questions can fuel lengthy debate, but regardless of the outcome of such discussions, practical implementation of any scheme of shared governance of the electoral process presents staggering difficulties.

Most politicians already worry about the press having too much power, so it's unlikely any candidate is going to agree to a systematic allocation of authority that formalizes the media's role. On the other hand, the public deserves more than a presentation of a succession of political faits accomplis, so politicians' power needs to be tempered somehow.

As complex as this matter may be, it's something journalists need to worry about. Too much passivity gives an edge to the politicians, and that advantage is likely to work against the public's interests.

Ethical questions usually arise not because of premeditated wrongdoing (such as accepting bribes) but because of laziness or negligence. When political journalists stumble in doing their jobs it probably is because they have not done their work with adequate thoroughness. That constitutes, in effect, a failure of ethical standards.

"Going Native" and Other Seductions

Another ethical problem that arises during campaigns has been called "going native." This happens when a journalist becomes too close to the candidate he is covering and becomes more a booster than a reporter.

In the course of a long campaign, when almost every waking hour is spent with the candidate and his staff, a reporter might decide he likes what he sees. If this happens, journalistic objectivity can suffer. When writing his story, the reporter might overlook a gaffe by the candidate or some other incident that casts a negative light on the campaign.

The politicians might foster a friendly relationship (either sincerely or with ulterior motives) as the campaign proceeds and the candidate, staff, and press corps become "one big happy family." The journalists begin seeing themselves as insiders rather than as representatives of the outsiders, the electorate.

The temptation to "go native" is one reporters face when they cover politicians they like or when they report on a part of government such as the Pentagon that appeals to patriotism and other loyalties. Some journalists who have spent years covering the Pentagon are said to have developed yearnings to wear uniforms themselves.

Subjects of news coverage sometimes don't understand the reporter's role. During the Vietnam War, one high-ranking military officer—exasperated by press coverage he considered "negative"—asked a reporter, "When are you going to get on the team?"

Resisting impulses to "get on the team" is one of a reporter's basic responsibilities. Becoming an agent for the person or institution being covered is the job of a public relations person, not a reporter.

Nor is it the job of the reporter to wage war against the subject of news coverage. Using a news medium to carry out a personal vendetta against a candidate whom a reporter dislikes is unethical, as is a reporter's attacking an issue or an institution based on his personal feelings.

Dispassion is more easily prescribed than achieved, particularly when a reporter finds himself covering a highly emotional subject.

For example, when covering the Democratic Convention in Chicago in 1968, some reporters were outraged by what they considered to be police brutality directed against demonstrators. The reporter's job, however, was not to editorialize about the conduct of the Chicago police, but rather to report what was happening. If people are fully and accurately informed, they can make their own decisions about right and wrong. Despite this ideal, however, not even the most stoic reporter could simply shrug off events in Chicago (especially because they came so soon after the assassinations of Martin Luther King and Robert Kennedy). Inevitably, some bitterness and sadness colored coverage of the 1968 campaign.

One ethical issue that sometimes arises during campaign coverage is rooted in the intense competitiveness of the news business itself. This is a product of a conscious or unconscious desire to be on "the winner's bus"; in other words, to be covering the candidate who apparently has the best chance of winning the election.

Frontrunning candidates get the most coverage. Reporters covering frontrunning candidates get the most exposure.

Television stories about a frontrunner will run almost every day and will receive maximum air time; the also-rans are covered sporadically and briefly. Newspaper articles about frontrunners appear on page one; reports about the other candidates' activities are buried in the back pages.

The "star system" that dominates principally (but not exclusively) the electronic media rewards reporters not just for enterprise and skill, but also, in effect, for luck.

For example, the television correspondent who finds the candidate he is covering leading the pack knows that as a reporter he has a potential gold mine. The increased visibility this reporter's stories will generate makes that reporter more of a star, which in turn is likely to be rewarded with more choice assignments and larger paychecks.

No real harm is done by these rewards of being on the winner's bus as long as it doesn't affect the way the reporter treats his subject. The danger is that a journalist might try to keep his candidate as the frontrunner by treating him more gently than he deserves.

Some reporters who covered the 1972 presidential primaries, when George McGovern transformed himself from long-shot to frontrunner, remember thinking that they "didn't want to spoil a story that good" and thus ignored some of the negative aspects of the McGovern campaign in favor of maintaining the Cinderella-type story of McGovern's miraculous climb to the nomination.

Such favoritism distorts the news and threatens the trust in the news media the public must have.

Jesse Jackson's 1984 campaign presented examples of a different kind of slanted coverage—one based less on favoritism than on uncertainty about how to treat the first major black presidential candidate.

How was Jackson covered—as a politician who had a reasonable chance of becoming president, or as a celebrity? If journalists believed he would not be the Democratic nominee (and almost all felt this way), why was the Jackson campaign covered so extensively? Alternatively, if reporters thought Jackson might win, why did they not more closely examine his lack of government experience, his sources of funding, and his ties to extremist supporters?

Jackson was grilled about his remarks referring to Jews as "Hymies" and New York as "Hymietown," and about his links to Nation of Islam leader Louis Farrakhan. But even this questioning was not as rugged as any other (white) candidate would have been subjected to had he made such comments or had such allies.

Another issue that arose for news organizations concerned assignments to cover Jackson. Should black reporters be given this job? Would this be racist, or merely the best way to get information from Jackson, who clearly was more forthcoming with black journalists?

Most of these questions were unresolved in 1984. Recognizing the historic nature of the Jackson candidacy and the race-related volatility inherent in this campaign, reporters proceeded gingerly.

That in itself was a mistake. Candidates for president should not be treated gingerly, and press uncertainties about policy are no excuse for doing so. Incomplete coverage is poor coverage. Bob Faw, the thoughtful CBS correspondent who covered Jackson during much of the 1984 race, said that news stories about Jackson tended to portray him as "a caricature at worst, a symbol at best." That kind of reporting provides an inadequate basis for voters to make rational decisions about a potential president's ability to govern the nation.

Jackson's style of campaigning added to reporters' difficulties. By far the most flamboyant candidate in 1984, with a flair for media events that could make even Ronald Reagan look like an amateur, Jackson truly commanded news coverage.

Examples of Jackson's events were his mission to Syria to negotiate the release of an American pilot who had been shot down over Lebanon, and his meeting with Fidel Castro to secure freedom for some Americans being held in Cuban prisons. In terms of making front pages or the network newscasts, these trips certainly outdistanced traveling to hog farms in Iowa with Walter Mondale. But what did they really mean? Would Jackson as president conduct American foreign policy solely on the basis of personal diplomacy. That's the kind of question that wasn't asked.

By 1987, when Jackson embarked on his next run for the presidency, press timidity had decreased slightly. Jackson ran this time as more of a mainstream candidate, acknowledging his need to broaden his base beyond the black electorate. This meant his choices of issues, speaking style, and audiences were changing. He was more like the other aspiring presidents and thus was easier to cover. Also, with one Jackson campaign behind them, political journalists were less timid in their reporting.

Predicting Election Results

Perhaps the most hotly debated ethical question about current news coverage of politics centers on the television networks' early predictions of election results.

Exit polling, not a crystal ball, is used as the basis for these forecasts. The developing science of exit polling is relatively simple. Certain precincts throughout the country are selected based on their population and their voting history, and in those precincts a certain number of voters are questioned as they leave their polling places.

The strength of this kind of polling is found in its logistics. Persons emerging from a voting booth are almost certainly actual voters; persons queried at home before an election (via telephone or in-person visit) might say how they plan to vote but then fail to do so. Proximity of the pollster to the voting place heightens the accuracy of the sample's responses.

When the responses of these voters are compared (usually by a computer) to past polling and to past vote results, projections can be made.

For example, if in Precinct X voters preferred Jimmy Carter by 55 percent to 45 percent for Ronald Reagan in 1980, but the sampled voters emerging from the polls in November, 1984, indicate they prefer Reagan to Walter Mondale by a 60 percent-40 percent margin, then that contrast is used as part of a complex calculation (again, by computer) of the likely outcome of that state's vote.

Polling is an increasingly precise science. The exit polls conducted by the networks can be assumed to be very reliable. But that is not the issue.

Suppose you are a voter living in California. You plan to vote after work, at about 6:00 P.M. That is 9:00 P.M. eastern time, which means most of the polls in both the eastern and central time zones have closed.

By the time you are preparing to go to your polling place the networks, based on their exit polling, are reporting who will end up with the eastern states' electoral votes. Also, based on exit polling conducted in California during the day, they can even tell you who will win your own state's electoral votes.

The danger of this occurs when the voter rationalizes: "If the networks say it's over, it's over. I'll just stay home and not bother to vote."

If this happens—if a news organization discourages someone from voting—then the news media are hampering the mechanics of the electoral process.

Press coverage throughout a campaign "influences outcomes" simply by informing voters about what is going on. But racing to report as early as possible the election day results is moving beyond the appropriate tasks of journalism.

No one knows for certain what impact early predictions have. In 1980, President Carter compounded the problem by conceding to Ronald Reagan while west coast polls were still open. By declaring the presidential race over, Carter implicitly discouraged many persons from bothering to vote. This might not have changed the eventual presidential outcome, but who knows how it affected the results of congressional, state, and local races?

In 1984, projections of the Reagan landslide again came as early as 8:00 P.M. eastern time (5:00 pacific time). Of course, based on polls conducted throughout the campaign that showed Reagan with a massive (and growing) lead, the Reagan victory had been taken for granted by almost all political observers. Most voters probably went to the polls fairly certain how the presidential race would turn out, so the networks' projections likely had little impact.

Not all journalists approve of this prediction game. For example, newspaper columnist Mike Royko has urged his readers to sabotage the process by lying to any exit pollsters they might encounter.

The centers of power within the news business, however, apparently approve of the polling aspect of election coverage. Executives of news organizations justify their use of early projections by saying their obligation is to report whatever news they have as soon as they have it. That is a simplistic approach to a complex issue and ducks some important questions.

First, is a public purpose served by these early projections? Probably not. Voters' curiosity may be satisfied and networks' clairvoyance aided, but the electorate gains little if any essential news. Would the public be harmed if they had to wait a few more hours to find out who won the election? Again, probably not.

Second, is electoral behavior—especially voter turnout—affected by the projections? Finding solid evidence about this is difficult, but it is reasonable to assume that some persons who had planned to vote decide not to when they are told what the election results will be.

Third, are the news media playing an appropriate role if their projections affect election results? In other words, when journalists make these projections do they cross the line between reporters and participants?

This transition in roles seems hard to deny. That it takes place in such an obvious way is perhaps an admission by news organizations that they truly are *actors* in the nation's political dramas.

Ethical questions arise almost daily. In political journalism the power of the news media is strikingly obvious. Electoral outcomes—and thus the course of the nation—are inevitably affected not just by election night reporting but by virtually every aspect of coverage of politicians and issues. This coverage is so heavily relied upon by voters that it is a principal factor in determining how someone will vote.

This tremendous power, for good or ill, will continue to be exercised. The journalists who wield it should have a firm ethical foundation on which to base their doing so. Journalists, like politicians, should be constantly tested regarding their adherence to standards.

7 | The Media Candidate—Covering Ronald Reagan

N ever has a politician used the media as successfully as has Ronald Reagan. Both as candidate and as officeholder, Reagan has used both news and paid media—particularly television—to build and fortify a remarkable political career. Whatever anyone's personal opinion about Reagan's policies or his competence, this president's skill at using mass media is unsurpassed.

Such talents do not appear spontaneously. Like other political attributes, they require years of cultivation. Reagan's career as an actor has served him well. He can deliver a line with the appropriate degree of conviction. He understands what the camera can do for him and do to him.

Transforming Hollywood skills into political assets isn't difficult. Reagan is not the first to do so: song-and-dance man George Murphy served in the United States Senate, and other stars have become involved in politics on behalf of various candidates and causes. At the very least, years on the movie screen can provide a level of name recognition that some aspiring candidates never attain.

Political Beginnings

Reagan's first nationally visible political foray occurred in 1964 when he put his charisma to work in a television spot on behalf of Republican presidential nominee Barry Goldwater.

90

Obviously, the spot didn't save Goldwater, but it served as a launching pad for Reagan. After Goldwater's massive defeat, the Republican Right was looking for a new champion, preferably someone who could handle himself in the increasingly important television arena. Reagan was a logical choice.

The transition from spokesman to candidate took place in the volatile environment of California politics. With his image as a "true believer" in the conservative cause, Reagan started out with a constituency. But it would take more than that to win a statewide election.

Reagan's first political race, for governor of California in 1966, was versus a powerful incumbent, Edmund "Pat" Brown. In 1962, Brown had disrupted Richard Nixon's political comeback by defeating the former vice president, precipitating Nixon's famous press conference in which he told reporters, "You won't have Dick Nixon to kick around any more."

Despite Brown's prowess as a giant-killer, Reagan beat him by almost a million votes, carrying many of the Democratic working class areas that Brown had won before.

In part, Reagan's victory can be ascribed to rising conservative sentiment, but probably more important was Reagan himself. The voters had their first glimpse of Reagan as candidate and they liked what they saw. Democratic Party leaders, looking back at the 1966 campaign, admitted underestimating Reagan's articulateness and the intangible personal appeal that won hearts and votes.

If voters had made their decisions solely on ideological grounds, Reagan might well have lost. Reagan, however, demonstrated a skill that has marked his career: he is a politician who doesn't seem to be a politician. He appeals to voters primarily as a human being, not as an ideologue.

In this first campaign, Reagan proved himself a formidable media candidate. Television is the ideal medium to capture superficial elements of personality. Affability can be transmitted via grins and waves of the hand, through a few off-the-cuff sentences, and in the carefully staged media event that showcases the candidate's strengths and obscures his weaknesses.

As a first-time candidate running against a knowledgeable incumbent, Reagan was able to find shelter in the brevity of television news stories. Reagan might not have been able to master all the issues facing California government, but he certainly could master an array of one-liners that conveyed the desired image of pleasant competence to the television audience.

Reagan's 1966 race and his successful gubernatorial re-election campaign in 1970 demonstrated his ability to effectively and consistently use television to complement his political skills.

In the midst of his California gubernatorial tenure, Reagan ventured gingerly into national politics. With uncharacteristic lack of political sensitivity, Reagan waded into the 1968 Republican National Convention, offering himself as a last-minute alternative to Richard Nixon.

By the time Reagan made this move, Nixon already had a solid grip on the nomination, so to Nixon and his allies, Reagan appeared an overly ambitious spoiler of party unity.

For Reagan, however, this apparently quixotic venture provided some subtle benefits. Reagan's tentative surfacing offered the national political press corps and the Republican activists from throughout the country a tantalizing glimpse of a candidate who would bide his time before making a serious run for the presidency.

The 1976 Campaign

When Reagan left the governor's office in January, 1975, after concluding his second term, he held a unique strategic position. His party was in shambles. Richard Nixon had resigned in disgrace and an untested Gerald Ford was president.

Ford had never run for office in an area larger than a congressional district. How Ford would fare in a national campaign was the subject of much speculation, especially among those who wanted to see Ronald Reagan become president.

Free from the responsibilities of the governorship, Reagan embarked on a media campaign that proved financially and politically valuable. Each week he made several speeches for an average fee of $5,000. His syndicated column appeared in 174 newspapers and his brief radio commentaries were carried by about 200 stations.

In addition to improving Reagan's personal finances, these efforts further established Reagan as the voice of the Republican Right, the heir to Barry Goldwater, and a clear alternative to moderate Gerald Ford and his newly named vice president, Nelson Rockefeller.

Reagan's "journalistic" activity was a new facet of a media candidacy. Other politicians have undertaken comparable efforts, but few, if any, have done so with the media-wise adroitness of Reagan.

Although the column and radio work ended when Reagan became a formal candidate, his early, pre-campaign maneuvering was aided substantially by this print and broadcast exposure. As he has done so often, Reagan was making the communications media work for him.

Despite Ford's inexperience in national politics, he was the incumbent president, and as such possessed enough power over Republican Party machinery to keep the nomination process tilted in his favor. But Reagan proved a formidable foe. After narrowly losing to Ford in the New Hampshire primary, Reagan and the President conducted a seesaw battle, with Reagan winning in some southern, midwestern, and western states, while Ford did well in delegate-heavy northern industrial states.

After 23 primaries (those races that were contested and in which the candidates' names appeared on the ballot), Reagan actually led in the number of votes received, but Ford narrowly gained a majority of convention delegates. At the GOP national convention in Kansas City, Ford received 1,187 delegate votes to 1,070 for Reagan.

Saddled with liabilities of the Nixon scandals and his own pardon of the former president, Ford was unable to withstand the skillful campaign of Jimmy Carter. Carter, who had displayed masterful understanding of the Democratic Party's nomination process, proved in the general election campaign that he could achieve remarkable political success by condemning "politics as usual."

(A media sidelight to the Ford-Carter race was the release of the film version of the best-selling book, *All the President's Men*. This movie, starring Robert Redford and Dustin Hoffman as *Washington Post* reporters Bob Woodward and Carl Bernstein, depicted the unraveling of the Watergate scandal and reminded voters of the ignominy of the recently departed Republican administration. This politically flavored entertainment certainly didn't help Ford.)

The bitterness engendered during the Republican primaries limited Reagan's willingness to assist Ford. Reagan spend most of the general election campaign as a spectator.

The 1980 Campaign

After Carter's victory over Ford, Reagan began contemplating strategy for another run for the White House. He resumed his newspaper and radio commentaries. This time he was not doing so to build name recognition; he no longer needed that. He wanted to keep himself in the coveted position of ascendant star—the man most likely to replace Ford as the leader of the Republican Party.

Press evaluations of Reagan's prospects were ambivalent. No one questioned Reagan's vote-getting prowess. His entire political career, capped by the barely unsuccessful challenge to Ford, had proved how dangerous it could be to underestimate his campaign skills.

On the other hand, by 1980 Reagan would by 69 years old and five years removed from the only elected office he had ever held. A certain skepticism still cropped up in considering a possible Reagan presidency. Was Ronald Reagan really anything more than a curiosity, a Hollywood charmer whose brief political career would be memorialized by an interesting footnote in political science textbooks?

The age issue shadowed Reagan's strategizing. Reagan's own pollsters were uncertain of the impact of their candidate's wrinkles. (This is the kind of issue about which persons being polled aren't always honest. As with questions related to race, many poll respondents often don't like to provide answers that sound prejudiced.)

By mid-1979, when numerous Republican contenders were preparing candidacies, press and politicians alike believed that Reagan could be beaten. According to the conventional wisdom, Jimmy Carter certainly was vulnerable, but to dethrone an incumbent would take more stamina than Reagan presumably possessed.

In the not-so-subtle world of media campaigning, Reagan's adversaries called attention to the age issue whenever possible. George Bush, for example, developed a great penchant for jogging, particularly when he could be accompanied by an entourage of news photographers.

Reporters covering Reagan when he announced his candidacy in November, 1979, and in the early months of 1980 saw the age issue as potentially devastating. Reagan's unimpressive early campaign speeches and his painfully obvious hearing problem (later corrected with a hearing aid) gave credence to the notion that time had passed Reagan by.

The early stages of presidential campaign are conducted in a much less formal atmosphere than prevails as election day draws near. Secret Service protection for non-incumbents doesn't begin until campaigning is well underway. Candidates, staff members, and reporters are gingerly getting to know each other. Freewheeling give and take between candidate and press often occurs on the campaign plane, in hotel bars, and at odd moments during the day's politicking.

Reagan never did well in such an unstructured relationship with the press. Even after years in the White House, Reagan still seems ill at ease when facing the avalanche of shouted questions that the assembled pack of reporters hurl at him whenever possible. As president, he has become fairly adroit at ducking those questions, responding with a smile, a wave, and a hand cupped around his ear whenever he doesn't want to answer. But in those early stages of the 1980 race, Reagan often seemed to be a nice old man who was having considerable difficulty understanding what was going on around him. Many reporters assumed voters would share this perception and turn their attention to other contenders.

In making this assumption, journalists committed the classic error in coverage of Ronald Reagan: They underestimated his ability to communicate with the electorate when given the opportunity to control the means of communication.

Put Reagan in front of a television camera and Teleprompter with a carefully crafted speech and he becomes a powerhouse. Thoughts of senility disappear after the first self-deprecating joke or the initial tear-jerking appeal to the audience's patriotism.

Mass communications media diminish some persons, stripping them of their personal qualities and rendering them cold caricatures of themselves. Other persons, such as Reagan, enhance their strengths, and make their political messages most palatable, through their ability to use communications technology.

In 1980, Reagan was almost knocked off his political track before he had a chance to put his media skills to work. Iowa's party caucuses, which receive more attention from the press than from the voters, were held in January, 1980. Reagan's strategists opted for a relatively low-profile campaign, with Reagan spending less time in the state than did several of his opponents.

With Reagan absent and with speculation rife about his ability and willingness to meet the demands of a national campaign, the press corps looked for other candidates on whom to focus attention. Enter George Bush.

Facing a horde of reporters starved for stories, Bush simply gave them something to write about. His Iowa campaign was well organized, he had adequate funding, his dappled career (congressman, CIA director, envoy to China, etc.) provided angles for stories about a variety of issues, and, most important, he was physically present. Of all the major candidates, Bush spent the most time in Iowa. He worked through the bitter Iowa winter, spending several weeks in the state just before the caucuses.

Like nature, the press abhors a vacuum. The campaign drama demanded players. Bush took the stage and held it, at least for a while.

Bush defeated Reagan narrowly in Iowa and instantly was proclaimed the frontrunner by much of the press corps. Reagan's loss in a strongly conservative midwestern state seemed to prove the theory that the old man had lost his touch. The Bush campaign rolled on to New Hampshire hoping to land a knockout punch in that state's February primary.

But no longer was Bush running against a phantom. Reagan came to New Hampshire and stayed, traveling by bus throughout the small state, popping up constantly in person and on local television.

Television provided Reagan with a vital boost in New Hampshire. A Reagan-Bush debate was to be held in Nashua. The Reagan campaign agreed to pay for the costs of staging the debate after negotiations with the Bush staff regarding funding broke down. Four other GOP presidential candidates showed up, protesting their exclusion from the debate. Reagan wanted to open up the format to include the others; Bush refused.

When Reagan, in his opening remarks, began to argue for including the others, the debate moderator, newspaper editor Jon Breen, told a technician to turn off Reagan's microphone. An angry Reagan grabbed the mike and said, "I paid for this microphone,

Mr. Green" (sic). The audience in the hall cheered Reagan, and the many other voters who saw this incident as a spot on newscasts saw an impressively crisp Reagan taking charge of a difficult situation. (A footnote to this incident: Almost the same line had been delivered in similar context by Spencer Tracy in the 1948 film, State of the Union.)

Debate protocol is not a particularly important matter, but in the few moments of this confrontation, Reagan proved that he still knew how to respond to a great cue line. When Breen challenged him, Ronald Reagan became John Wayne (or at least Spencer Tracy). George Bush remained George Bush.

This incident by no means determined the outcome of the New Hampshire race, but it certainly put to rest the notion that Reagan lacked the energy or will to fight for the nomination. On February 26, Reagan received 51 percent of the New Hampshire Republican vote; Bush garnered 22 percent. (Howard Baker finished third with 13 percent. The rest of the vote was scattered among several other candidates.)

Many of the political reporters who had been so quick to write off Reagan after the Iowa loss now were grasping for explanations of Reagan's strength.

Reagan had two tremendous assets Bush could not match. First, Reagan had been moving towards the Republican presidential nomination ever since his Goldwater speech in 1964. Loyalties to Reagan ran deep among conservatives; the Reagan constituency in New Hampshire had been cultivated for years and was ready to be summoned. Bush, on the other hand, was starting from scratch.

Second, the greatest strength of any Reagan campaign always has been Reagan himself. When he appears in person or on television, he communicates a potent personality that captures the attention of voters. In New Hampshire, unlike in Iowa, Reagan used this asset and maintained high visibility.

The contest with Bush turned out to be a see-saw battle that continued for several months. Every time Bush seemed to be finally out of the race, he would score another primary win and keep his campaign alive.

During these months, the Reagan staff assiduously courted the press. Given Reagan's propensity for generating unnecessary controversy through his off-the-cuff remarks, the Reagan staff faced the classic media manager's task: Show off the candidate in the best possible light without letting the press get too close, too often.

Reporters aren't stupid. They know when they are being "massaged" by politicians and generally they resent it, sometimes lashing back with particularly nasty coverage if they feel the attempts at manipulation are excessive.

That the Reagan staff was so successful in influencing coverage of their candidate was more a tribute to their skill than it was a sign that reporters weren't doing their jobs. Throughout the primary season, Reagan press aides and issues experts were readily available to correspondents. Interviews with Reagan could be scheduled even by local print and broadcast journalists.

Good will didn't have much to do with Reagan's accessibility. He wanted exposure and he needed the press to give it to him. A flaw in Reagan's campaign strategy made this reliance on the press even more important.

Thinking that Reagan would lock up the nomination early in 1980, his campaign managers spent heavily in late 1979 and the first months of the election year. They soon found themselves approaching the federal limit on campaign spending, but Bush's tenacity kept the nomination just out of reach.

(Those campaign leaders were fired by Reagan on the day of the New Hampshire primary and replaced with tough financial managers. The handling of this matter was yet another example of Reagan's shrewd press strategy. Normally, firing a campaign manager would generate much coverage, most likely making the candidate look none too good. But because the "executions" took place on election day, news of the voting swamped coverage of the internal campaign matters.)

Faced with fiscal constraints on the amount of advertising they could purchase, the Reagan strategists had to rely heavily on the free visibility news coverage provided.

The staff-reporter relationship in the Reagan campaign often was surprisingly friendly. Despite widely held perceptions that the press corps is dominated by liberals, many reporters grew to like Reagan personally (based on what little they saw of him) and found his staff cooperative and competent, which was more than could be said for the aides of other candidates (including some of Jimmy Carter's White House staff members).

As the campaign progressed, however, Reagan needed the press less than they needed him. By the time he became the nominee, Reagan *had* to be covered every day, so the nature of the symbiosis changed. By the latter stages of the general election campaign, reporters were complaining publicly about Reagan's refusal to talk with them. Necessity, not benevolence, generally dictates the extent of access reporters will have to a candidate.

The beginning of the 1980 general election campaign saw a reversal of the parties' fortunes from those in 1976. This time it was the Democrats who had the fractious convention, with Jimmy Carter and Edward Kennedy sniping at each other throughout the New York sessions. The Republicans, meanwhile, engaged in a love feast in Detroit. Reagan and his conservative allies took firm control of the party and pacified moderates by nominating George Bush for vice president.

National conventions for the most part have become media events that the parties use to showcase their candidates with as much glitter as they can devise. In terms of substantive debate or hard news, the conventions are fairly barren.

But the spirit of the convention sets the tone for the coming campaign. A party that slices itself apart during its primaries and then fails to heal during the convention will spend valuable campaign time negotiating internal peace, as evidenced by the Republicans in 1976, when the Ford-Reagan battle in Kansas City was never wholly resolved. The Democrats faced the same problem in 1980: Carter had to rally his troops while Reagan rolled steadily from the convention into his campaign.

The influence of the news media, particularly television, loomed large throughout the 1980 campaign. Carter and Reagan both were seasoned campaigners; both understood the enormous power of the 90-second slices of campaign life that reached the public via the networks' newscasts.

With the benefit of hindsight, perhaps the most influential news coverage was not that of the campaign itself, but rather of the issue that cast a shadow over American life for more than a year: the Iran hostage crisis.

As the Carter administration followed a tortuous path towards securing release of the Americans held hostage in the United States embassy in Tehran, the news media covered the process in excruciating detail. With its proclivity for reducing even the most complicated issues to boxscore-type reporting, television news, like some mournfully deep-sounding bell, tolled the days of diplomatic failure.

Certainly, the news media didn't create the hostage crisis or the Carter administration's problems in addressing it, but these daily reminders of American impotence certainly affected the voters' opinions about Carter's competence.

This news coverage also made it less necessary for Reagan to engage in what might have appeared unseemly criticism of American foreign policy in a time of crisis. He could let the news media do it for him.

The Iran crisis also posed a potential problem for Reagan. Republican strategists' greatest fear was about an "October surprise"—a dramatic release of the hostages that suddenly would make Carter a hero. Reagan's aides could worry about this and could talk to reporters about how unscrupulously self-serving such a Carter maneuver might be, but they could do nothing to actually provide for such an event. This is one of the perils of running against an incumbent president.

Reagan's polls in mid-October showed him leading Carter by roughly six percentage points, but fear of a last-minute Carter comeback spurred Reagan to seek a televised debate with the President.

The debate was held in Cleveland on October 28, just a week before the November 4 election. As has been the case with most of these showdowns, this was less a debate than it was a joint press conference, with each candidate offering carefully rehearsed responses to easily anticipated questions from a panel of journalists.

The debate demonstrated the relative television skills of the two candidates. Carter demonstrated impressive command of complex issues, but came across as steely and cold. Reagan didn't try to rattle off numbers in response to Carter's precision, but instead cast himself in the role of raconteur, relaxed and affable.

The single line most remembered from this debate was Reagan's response to Carter's charge that Reagan had opposed Medicare: "There you go again." Carter's allegation was fundamentally accurate, but Reagan sidestepped the substance of the matter and adopted the pose of beleaguered statesman being unfairly harassed.

This line was no spur-of-the-moment thought. It had occurred to

Reagan during his lengthy rehearsals for the debate and he stored it away, waiting for the right instant to use it.

The 1980 debate served Reagan's purposes much the same way the 1976 Ford-Carter debate had helped Carter. Reagan did nothing spectacular, but he did erase some negative images by not appearing senile or sounding like a bomb-thrower. He was able to stand face-to-face with the President of the United States and come away looking like his equal.

Reagan's strength in the debate opened floodgates of support. During the final week of the campaign, his polls showed him climbing steadily. Doubts about Reagan's being adequately "presidential" had apparently been substantially reduced by the debate.

The debate also underscored fundamental differences in the ways Reagan and Carter used mass media to appeal to the electorate. In 1976, voters fed up with scandal were willing to gamble that Carter's moral cleanliness and new perspective would overcome his governmental inexperience.

By 1980, Carter no longer could speak as an outsider and blame the failures of government on others. The high-sounding rhetoric of 1976—"a government as good as its people," "I'll never lie to you," and so on—would ring false coming from a besieged incumbent. The righteousness imbued in Carter's pre-presidential speeches sounded preachy, not inspirational, after a few years had passed.

Carter's 1980 campaign speeches contained a share of Calvinism that sometimes backfired, particularly when Carter was perceived as personally attacking Reagan. For example, in early October, Carter gave a speech in which he warned that the election would determine "whether Americans might be separated, black from white, Jew from Christian."

This speech resulted in an interesting turnabout. The press jumped on Carter for being unnecessarily nasty and engaging in unprincipled scare tactics. Carter found himself in the strange position of an incumbent president having to apologize for his rhetoric (doing so in a televised interview with Barbara Walters). Reagan, meanwhile, simply shook his head with statesmanlike sadness and lamented that the campaign had descended to such depths. In this minor flap, Reagan looked more presidential than did the President.

In his television appearances throughout the campaign, Reagan was able to set precisely the tone he wanted. His vigorous presentations in front of the camera took care of the age issue. His declarations of resolve in the face of terrorism and Soviet expansionism sounded tough, but not dangerous, particularly to Americans who felt humiliated by the Iranian ayatollahs.

Beyond policy matters, Reagan established himself as the more likable candidate. He was the one you might want to sit with at the corner tavern, have a few beers, and talk over old times. Carter seemed more likely to march into the tavern to deliver a temperance lecture.

The extent to which voting behavior is affected by this kind of affection is hard to measure, but it probably is substantial. Once the voter passes a judgmental threshold—deciding that both candidates are competent enough to do no serious damage—then the more intangible factors take over. After all, the act of voting is basically an expression of trust, and trust is determined largely by instinct.

Inspiring that trust is something Ronald Reagan has done superbly throughout most of his political career. Perhaps it is the grandfatherly demeanor he exudes (similar to the image some ascribe to Walter Cronkite), or some delicate balance of mannerisms, rhetoric, and charm. Whatever the formula, it works remarkably well.

Carter lacked such magnetism. Few voters hated Carter personally; they didn't see him as corrupt (like Nixon), lazy, or in any other way purposely working against their interests. They might even have forgiven him his apparently limited competence if they had liked him more or not liked his opponent so much. But the image Reagan projected and the image most voters wanted were virtually identical.

On November 4, the Reagan phenomenon became manifest in a landslide. Reagan beat Carter by more than eight million votes (out of roughly 90 million cast), receiving 50.7 percent of the votes to Carter's 41 percent and independent candidate John Anderson's 6.6 percent. The electoral vote margin was even more lopsided: Reagan 489, Carter 44.

Many elements shaped the Reagan victory: the hostage crisis, severe inflation, the energy shortage, and Carter's perceived flaws all hurt the incumbent. But in addition to skillfully underscoring

the negatives of the Carter administration, Reagan also successfully sold himself not as a lesser of evils but as a positive, forceful
leader.

The First Term

Riding the crest of this imagery, Reagan became president on
January 20, 1981, while on the same day the American hostages—
so much a factor during the campaign—were released from Iran.

The transition from candidate to president is never easy. Criticism and promises must give way to actual performance. The flash
and dazzle of campaigning yield to the tedious chore of making the
government work.

Or so the theory goes. To a certain extent, every president car-
ries with him into the White House vestiges of the campaign flair
that won the job in the first place. Presidents are successful only if
they appreciate the political nature of their job. They must seek
continuing support for their policies just as they sought votes.

Some presidents have not done particularly well at this. Despite
Jimmy Carter's brilliant pre-nomination strategy and his efficient
campaign versus Gerald Ford, he was remarkably ineffective as a
political leader once he became president.

Carter's forlorn appraisal of the country in his famous "malaise"
speech of July, 1979, failed in two ways: not only did it seem to
blame the American people for the country's problems, but it also
failed to suggest aggressive ways to resolve those problems. (Despite the "malaise" label attached to this speech, that word never
was used. Carter referred instead to a "crisis of confidence" striking
at the "very heart and soul and spirit of our national will.")

Reagan used Carter's political failings against him during the
1980 campaign and was determined not to make the same errors
during his own presidency. Reagan understood that the talents that
had carried him to the White House were the same skills that could
keep him there.

However history appraises the substance of the Reagan administration—the tax cuts, the invasion of Grenada, the talks with
Gorbachev, and other major issues—the form of the Reagan presidency certainly will merit much admiring study. Errors were made

on occasion (such as the Bitburg cemetery visit in 1984), but for the most part Reagan used the presidency as the "bully pulpit" Theodore Roosevelt had described and never lost sight of the need to maintain popular support for his policies. Until he slammed into the Iran-contra scandal that came to a head in 1987, Reagan seemed to lead a charmed political life.

Reagan knew that he himself was his administration's greatest asset. His personal popularity was such that it seemed able to overwhelm any foe. Whether stating his case in a televised speech or twisting arms in one-on-one lobbying, Reagan often proved irresistible. Match-ups against the likes of Senator Edward Kennedy or House Speaker Tip O'Neill were no contest. Public trust, that intangible but invaluable asset, was a political tool Reagan could use like a hammer.

Reagan's ability to make this trust work for him earned him the title (although used somewhat snidely by reporters) of "the great communicator." The President's forte was the televised speech.

The intimacy provided by a tight camera shot of Reagan at his Oval Office desk was nothing new. Other presidents had used the same format; Jimmy Carter even tried donning a sweater and delivering a true "fireside chat." Reagan's effectiveness, however, stemmed from things not visible to his audience, such as a Teleprompter (used, but not as effectively, by other presidents) from which he could read splendidly, using his actor's training to convincingly "sell" his message.

Reagan also saw to it that his speeches were understandable to virtually everyone in his audience. Sprinkling his presentations with anecdote and reminiscence, and even some White House-generated animated charts, Reagan was more storyteller than speechmaker.

The political effect of Reagan's efforts was remarkable. When Reagan asked for pressure to be put on Congress to help pass a bill, the letters and telegrams poured in. Congressmen taking soundings in their districts found that Reagan's credibility was high, and that to oppose him would take work, perhaps more work than voting against him was worth.

With this kind of support, Reagan proved remarkably successful in his first-term dealings, even with the Democrat-controlled House of Representatives.

Reagan's television appearances were not, however, flawless. The President had clear difficulties with the televised news conference. Here he had no Teleprompter, no control over subject matter, and often, apparently, no prepared answers for the questions he was asked.

For his ability to use television effectively, Reagan has been compared to President John Kennedy. Kennedy, however, was the unparalleled master of the televised news conference. He could retain large amounts of information and spew them forth when needed, he was fast enough on his feet to duck questions he didn't want to answer, he could use humor to deflect tough questions or lighten the tone of the press conference, and overall he was able to make the news conference a showcase for himself and his policies.

Reagan has never seemed as comfortable as Kennedy was during these sessions. On the advice of former President Richard Nixon and others, Reagan began preparing for news conferences much more carefully. He began studying, on his own and with his staff, two days before the news conference. Just before the session began, Reagan would scan the room via a television monitor to see which reporters were sitting where.

Also, Reagan came to recognize a kinship between the news conference and the campaign debate: What he said wasn't as important as how he said it, and his principal audience was not the assembly of reporters in the room with him, but rather the vast audience sitting in front of their television screens. As long as Reagan could gear his performance to the interests of this mass audience, the news conference could serve his purposes.

Soon Reagan was able to win at least passing grades for his performance. But protective aides and Reagan himself knew the news conference was not this president's best field on which to fight the battle for public opinion. Such formal sessions were scheduled infrequently; Reagan relied more on speeches, either from the Oval Office or on the road.

The essence of political communication is control of subject matter and format. Reagan was not about to surrender that control, no matter how loudly the White House press corps complained about the shortage of news conferences.

Reagan was able to convince people to trust him and thus accept his policies; he sold himself first and his issues second. This was playing to strength, a shrewd decision. Polls throughout Reagan's first term consistently showed Reagan's personal ratings higher than those for his policies. As Walter Mondale was to learn in 1984, pointing out problems with Reagan administration actions was not enough to shake the foundation of the administration's political support: Reagan himself.

A tragic incident early in Reagan's first term reinforced the President's popularity and underscored the potency of mass media. On March 30, 1981, after delivering a speech at the Washington Hilton Hotel, Reagan was shot by a deranged young drifter on the sidewalk outside the hotel. Reagan was struck once, by a deflected bullet that lodged an inch from his aorta. Reagan's press secretary, James Brady, a Secret Service agent, and a Washington policeman were also wounded.

Effective Secret Service procedure, superb medical care, and good luck saved Reagan's life. Facing his emergency with calmness and a spate of one-liners (to his wife, "I forgot to duck," and to emergency room personnel, "Please tell me you're Republicans"), Reagan himself measured up to the heroic ideals he had espoused during his campaign. To many Americans, this proved once and for all that Reagan was not merely an actor programmed to say "the right things," but truly was an inspiring leader.

The outpouring of sympathy and admiration for Reagan was enhanced by television's intense coverage of the shooting and its aftermath. The nature of television news technology has reached a remarkable state: Within 30 minutes of the gunfire on the Hilton sidewalk, every American with access to a television set could see the president of the United States being shot.

That is both wondrous and horrible. It is a tribute to the information-providing capabilities of the television networks and it is a grim commentary on what constitutes a nation-unifying event.

Regardless of questions of taste and some errors of news judgment (such as the inaccurate reports that White House press secretary Brady had died of his bullet wound), television involved the American people in the minute-by-minute drama of the President's fight for life. By bringing viewers so close to the event, television heightened its audience's intensity of feeling for the President.

Not surprisingly, Reagan's personal popularity rose substantially in polls taken soon after the assassination attempt. Given the controversy surrounding much of his domestic policy, especially his economic reform measures, this popularity could not be expected to last without careful nurturing of public opinion. These efforts were aimed not only at winning support for administration policies, but also at paving the way for Reagan's 1984 re-election campaign.

Of all Reagan's aides, the one who had most impact on the Reagan image as projected by the news media was not his press secretary, but rather the assistant White House chief of staff, Michael Deaver. A long-time Reagan loyalist, Deaver began his political career in the California statehouse and was well liked by both Ronald and Nancy Reagan.

To Deaver was entrusted the "look" of the Reagan presidency. For a chronicle of a president's activities, most Americans rely on brief nightly news video clips. The impression those one or two minutes leave does much to create predispositions of favor or dislike towards the president. Always conscious of camera angles and situations that would show his boss in the best possible light, Deaver directed events ranging from singer Michael Jackson's visit to the White House to more grandiose matters, such as the moving ceremonies on the cliffs overlooking the Normandy beaches, where Reagan spoke on the fortieth anniversary of D-Day. Deaver's influence was so pervasive that "leave it to Deaver" became the standard approach to White House events.

Although Deaver respected Reagan's ability to charm anyone and to come up with an appropriate one-liner in any situation, spontaneity was rare in Deaver-directed events. Total control was deemed essential to ensure just the right visuals and just the right timing to produce those few minutes of invaluable television time.

Deaver was not considered an ideologue. He left issues to other Reagan aides. He understood that the form as well as the substance of a presidency was important in maintaining the public support for the president as a person, and by extension, the president's policies.

If Deaver's work was manipulation, it didn't draw much resistance from the White House press corps. Although neither reporters nor Deaver would readily admit it, their goals were much the same: to generate the good video that would hold an audience's attention. By providing the press a steady stream of media events, Deaver limited the need for reporters to dig up stories on their own. The press' appetite for news can sometimes be sated if the volume of material is high, even if true news value is low.

The influential role played by Deaver is further evidence of the modern presidency's reliance on television and of the importance a president must attach to eliciting favorable news coverage. In many ways, little evolution occurred between the strategies of Reagan's 1980 campaign and his approach to the presidency. Whether winning votes or maintaining support for his administration, Reagan stayed with the tactics that had proved successful throughout his career.

The 1984 Campaign

As the 1984 campaign approached, Reagan and his closest supporters had good cause for optimism. The high unemployment rates that marred Reagan's first two years in office were declining. The public was wary about Reagan's foreign policy in the Middle East, Central America, and in relations with the Soviet Union, but no cutting issue (such as the Vietnam War or the Iran hostage crisis had been) seemed likely to cost Reagan votes. Reagan's personal popularity remained intact and the Republicans were as united as any political party is ever likely to be.

The Democrats, meanwhile, seemed intent on self-destruction. Former Vice President Walter Mondale saw his frontrunner status turn to ashes when Senator Gary Hart began winning primaries. Jesse Jackson's entry into the Democratic contest shook the already fragile coalition the Democrats would need if they were to have a chance against Reagan.

By the time Mondale claimed the nomination at the Democrats' San Francisco convention, he was in the unenviable position of having to play catch-up. Even the dramatic selection of Geraldine Ferraro as Mondale's running mate seemed unlikely to close the gap between Mondale and Reagan.

The Republicans knew it was their race to lose; they had the money, organization, and momentum to hold the White House if they didn't do anything disastrously stupid.

The GOP strategy was much the same as it had been in 1980; to let Ronald Reagan himself, rather than party or policies, dominate the campaign. Mondale could easily be tarred with the brush of the

Carter administration, so Reagan could still ask: "Aren't you better off today than you were four years ago? Don't you want to avoid turning back to chaotic days of the Carter regime?"

For the most part, Reagan played it safe in 1984. He asked for a vote of confidence in the course he had set, but he had no need to make controversial new proposals. He could appeal to generalized virtues, such as patriotism and family values, claiming them as his own. (This drove the Democrats to distraction. At their San Francisco convention, delegates were given American flags to wave in front of the television cameras so "we can take the flag back from Reagan." Reagan, unperturbed, continued his patriotic rhetoric.)

The Republican National Convention in Dallas symbolized the tone and technique of the Reagan battle plan. Since the platform was largely dictated by the White House and the nomination process was merely a matter of form, the delegates had little substantive business to transact. Thus, the convention became a campaign showcase, a week of free television advertising.

Even the convention hall rostrum was designed to meet demands of television. For easier television viewing, warm earth tones replaced the traditional red, white, and blue. Speeches were interspersed with expensively produced video pieces that might not have held the attention of delegates in the cavernous hall, but offered "real television" to the home audience.

The most effective of these videos was a 20-minute tribute to Reagan that included excerpts from his June speech at Normandy and personal reflections from the President and his wife. Within the convention hall, at least, this video had its desired effect: it enthralled delegates and brought tears to the eyes of many.

The Reagan video also turned out to be controversial. The networks finally protested about providing the Republicans with what amounted to free commercials. Although it could be argued that the entire convention coverage was more advertising than news, CBS and ABC drew the line at airing the Reagan tape. Only NBC ran it in its entirety when it was shown to the convention.

This gesture by the two networks didn't accomplish much, but it perhaps established a precedent for future convention coverage. Most of what goes on at a party convention is neither interesting nor newsworthy. The networks, local broadcast stations, and the print media spend millions on covering what often turns out to be a non-event. The principal beneficiary of this attention is the political party.

Gavel-to-gavel coverage of conventions probably could be eliminated with no loss to the public. The principal speeches and the nomination roll call contain the meat of the news generated by the convention, and live broadcast of these events usually would be sufficient. On occasions of battles over important platform planks, extra coverage could be offered.

The political parties probably would strongly object to this loss of air time. They have grown used to having their conventions showcased. Of course, the print media would still provide detailed coverage, but reliance on television has grown so great that politicians are unlikely to consider this an adequate substitute for live television.

Moving out of their safe, bland convention, the Republicans awaited Mondale's attacks. The Democratic ticket seemed to embody a combination of traditional liberalism (Mondale) and the politics of the future (Ferraro). That look, however, never took the tangible form of a campaign theme with which voters could identify. The Democrats clearly were against Reagan, but what were they for?

While the Republicans embraced such catchphrases as, "Stronger, Prouder, Better," the Democrats foundered. Mondale, after a long career in elective office, certainly had ideas about what he would do as president, but these ideas never emerged as the nuggets voters could easily consume.

In media-oriented politics, having good ideas isn't enough; those ideas must be put in a form compatible with media coverage. Even a brilliant candidate with magnificent ideas for his country must conform to this kind of format or risk his policies never receiving adequate consideration.

Mondale might or might not have been brilliant, but if he was, his campaign certainly didn't show it. His attacks on the Reagan administration seemed to have little effect, and the luster of the Ferraro nomination was tarnished by the prolonged investigation of her family's finances.

Facing a massive deficit in the polls, Mondale had to hope he could rescue his campaign in televised debates with Reagan. He almost did.

The first of two debates between the presidential contenders took place in Louisville on October 7. Mondale had to his advantage the history of underdogs and non-incumbents proving themselves "presidential" in these confrontations. Reagan brought with him his reputation for invincibility in front of the television camera.

For reasons that remain unclear, Reagan opened the debate by trying to do the things he does worst: relying on statistics rather than anecdotes, talking about detailed policy matters rather than sweeping philosophical values. By wading into such unfamiliar territory, Reagan put himself immediately on the defensive.

In what seemed a remarkable role reversal, Mondale concentrated on explaining the differences between his and Reagan's visions of America. Letting Reagan try to make his statistics comprehensible, Mondale relied on rhetorical flourishes that were rooted in New Deal philosophy and were designed to portray Reagan as isolated and uncaring.

Even when Reagan tried to return to his 1980 form with "There you go again," the response that had undermined Jimmy Carter, Mondale was ready for him. Mondale asked Reagan if he recalled when he had used that line before. Reagan looked baffled and just muttered. Mondale persisted in his attack, saying that Reagan had used that line to deflect Carter's accusation that Reagan wanted to cut Medicare and then, said Mondale, when Reagan assumed the presidency that is precisely what he tried to do. After this exchange, Reagan appeared totally out of energy.

Although Mondale seemed vague at many points in the debate, he appeared the victor because he seemed the more energetic and more incisive of the two. On a few issues, such as abortion, the ideological differences between Reagan and Mondale were clearly drawn, but for the most part the debate never rose above exchanges of generalities and gross misstatements of fact by both men.

Of course, debate coaches don't determine who "wins" a presidential debate. The voter sitting at home does, and if you are that voter, you receive substantial impetus in your decision-making from the way the news media report the debate.

In this case, the focus of much post-debate coverage was the "age issue." Responding to Mondale, Reagan looked, at best, ill at ease, and at worst, thoroughly confused. Some of the President's answers rambled, and they were filled with non sequiturs and factual errors.

To all but the most devoted Reagan fans, questions had to exist about the President's ability to function under pressure.

Reagan's performance might have been discounted as being nothing more than a one-night aberration had not the news media paid so much attention to it. For newscasts reporting the debate, the 90-minute event had to be boiled down to two or three minutes, with several brief soundbites to illustrate what reporters judged to be the most salient points.

Probably the most frequently used soundbites were Mondale's riposte to Reagan's "There you go again" and one of Reagan's incomprehensible rambles about Social Security. If you watched these newscasts, regardless of whether you had seen the debate, you probably were struck by how much Reagan looked like a tired old man and how Mondale, in comparison, seemed to embody vigor.

Watching post-debate analyses and the next day's news programs, you could see these supposedly representative moments (removed as they were from the context of the entire debate) several times. When coupled with reporters' comments about the growing consensus among politicians that Mondale had "won" the debate, these excerpts tended to confirm doubts about Reagan's performance.

Notably absent from most debate analyses was consideration of the substance of the candidates' positions on the issues raised by the panel's questions. Little notice was given to Reagan versus Mondale as Republican versus Democrat or conservative versus liberal. Listening to the two candidates discuss school prayer, abortion, or budget priorities in the debate revealed far more substantive differences than did those matters of style that captured most analysts' attention.

Follow-up stories about the debate demonstrated the news media's propensity to create self-fulfilling prophecies. Immediately after the debate, many journalists proclaimed it a Mondale victory. For the next several days, news reports told of the benefits Mondale was reaping as a result of his triumph—larger crowds at his rallies, a new confidence within the Democratic campaign.

Was this improvement in Mondale's prospects the product of the debate itself or of bullish news reports that generated a bandwagon effect? Both probably contributed to the Mondale upswing, but more so, this debate coverage exemplifies how news stories, particularly when they repeat the same theme for several days, can become more significant than the original event.

Reagan found himself in the unusual position of underdog as he prepared for the second debate. He still held a solid lead in the polls, but even his own supporters wondered if he could survive a disastrous performance in round two versus Mondale.

Preparation for these high stakes debates has become something of a science. The tools of the trade include special briefing books, rehearsals with stand-ins for the opponents (budget director David Stockman was cast as Reagan's foe), "pepper drills" of rapid-fire questions to test instinctive responses, plus an array of technical refinements involving lighting, make-up, and camera positioning.

Sometimes this preparation can be overdone. Nancy Reagan, among others, felt that Reagan had been tutored too much before the first debate and had become so concerned about remembering all he had been taught that the "real Reagan" never emerged. For debate number two, the plan was to "let Reagan be Reagan."

Mondale, for his part, knew he had to deliver a knockout punch in the debate. He had done well in Louisville, establishing himself as someone who could hold his own with Reagan, but he still faced the task of giving voters a reason to send Reagan into retirement. This second debate, scheduled for October 21 in Kansas City, would be Mondale's last chance to work a miracle.

Whatever Mondale's expectations may have been, they vanished quickly. The Democratic challenger looked terrible when the camera first focused on him; the studio lighting accentuated dark bags under his eyes. Mondale's appearance undermined his case as a vigorous alternative to Reagan.

Also, Mondale never pressed Reagan particularly hard. He let the President's misstatements go unchallenged and concentrated on explaining his own issues positions. That might have strengthened Mondale's image, but his principal mission on this night was to discredit Reagan. He made little headway on this.

Reagan, meanwhile, was holding his own. Aside from offering to share American "star wars" technology with the Soviet Union, he said little of interest. But he didn't blunder; he didn't appear incompetent. As the defending champion, all Reagan really had to do was avoid being knocked out.

Appropriately, the most remembered moment of the second debate was a Reagan one-liner. One of the questioners finally brought the age issue into the open, asking the President if he thought his age might impair his ability to govern. Reagan's response: "I want you to know I will not make age an issue of this campaign. I am not going to exploit for political purposes my opponent's youth and inexperience."

Even Mondale laughed, although he must have realized the devastating effect this one weak joke would have. Pollsters monitoring audience reaction to the debate found that Reagan scored heavily with this light-hearted response. He had put to rest what probably was the most dangerous issue the Democrats could raise.

Few people seemed to notice that Reagan's closing remarks in the debate were barely coherent and that he had to be interrupted by the moderator after using his allotted time without reaching a conclusion. The joke was to be the dominant soundbite, the nugget shining throughout the follow-up news coverage.

In many ways it was fitting that Reagan's final electoral victory should be ensured by a triumph of personality. The disarming charm that had proved such an asset throughout his political career came to the fore one more time. Mondale, the conventional politician, relied on conventional political strategy, trying to debate ideology and issues.

As the 1984 debates proved, modern news coverage, particularly that provided by television, is better suited to Reagan's approach. Personality survives compression better than does philosophy. Rare is the soundbite that runs more than 30 seconds; rare is the issue that can be articulated with such brevity.

Reagan's technique as media politician had changed little between 1980 and 1984, although he had picked up some assets along the way. As the incumbent, Reagan could remain comfortably aloof from the political press corps. He also could enjoy the trappings of his office, such as Air Force One, the Secret Service, a staff of skilled logistical planners, and the information-gathering machinery of the executive branch.

Republican campaign strategists, however, did not want to overly protect Reagan. He was not like a Richard Nixon, whose coldness was best kept at a distance from the voters. Reagan on the campaign trail was invaluable to the vote-getting process. His appearances combined the grandeur of the presidency with the personal appeal of a benign hero. These campaign events were, of course, geared to reach both immediate and remote audiences.

For example, emerging from the shambles of the first debate, Reagan embarked on a whistle-stop railroad trip through the Midwest. This seemed an old-fashioned kind of campaigning, with voters turning out at cities and crossroads as Reagan slowly made his way through the American heartland where he could expect solid support.

These voters enjoyed seeing their candidate, but the real audience for this trip was voters who lived thousands of miles away from the railroad procession. These were the people who would see two-minute packages depicting the journey, complete with helicopter shots of the train wending its way across the midwestern farmland.

Such images reinforced Reagan's strengths: Here he was the traditionalist, apparently forsaking the slickness and high-pressured environment of the debate and returning to the roots of American politics.

This controlled, remote view of the campaign was a bit fuzzy; the news stories were montages of Reagan quips and flags waving. It was a different picture and a different candidate than what the cold studio cameras had depicted during the debate. These images washed away some of the painful impressions created by Reagan's debate performance.

Such ability to shift gears, to swiftly reclaim the advantage in the battle for public loyalties was a Reagan trademark. In 1976, when Gerald Ford had suffered at Jimmy Carter's hands in a debate, Ford spent precious days trying to explain his way out of trouble. Reagan simply moved on, knowing that voters' attention would move with him.

To a considerable extent, a forceful candidate such as Reagan can dictate the pace of the campaign and carry the public's focus with him. The press would cover Reagan, whatever he was doing. If he spent time licking his wounds after the first debate, the press would report that and give voters more time to ponder Reagan's poor performance. If he moved ahead aggressively, news stories would be about what he was doing at the moment. The debate would become old news.

This kind of damage control has its limits. Reagan certainly was hurt by the first debate and needed to recoup in the second meeting. But he and his staff did not allow the campaign to be untracked by the initial negative news coverage. They forced the press to move along.

Reagan had been called the "teflon president" because nothing bad ever seemed to stick to him. That certainly was the case during this campaign. Mondale never was able to create enough faith in his own abilities or enough doubt about Reagan's skills to make the presidential campaign of 1984 much of a contest.

The result: a phenomenal landslide. Reagan received 59 percent of the popular vote and 525 electoral votes to Mondale's 41 percent and 13 electoral votes. (Mondale carried only his home state of Minnesota and the District of Columbia.)

Lessons from the First Reagan Term

As candidate and president, Ronald Reagan demonstrated how a forceful, media-wise leader can affect the balance of power between the news media and politicians. After news coverage helped speed Richard Nixon's departure from office, and in light of the damage done to Gerald Ford's and Jimmy Carter's careers by press-exacerbated wounds, this fragile relationship had seemed increasingly imbalanced.

Only rarely did the press cry "foul" because of treatment by the Reagan administration. (One instance was the exclusion of reporters from the invasion of Grenada.) Reporters might not have liked their limited access to the president or the administration's overuse of media events, but never did such matters reach the point at which public opinion swung behind the press' position. Reagan knew just how far he could carry the adversarial relationship.

Also, Reagan was usually able to keep control of the national agenda. There are times, such as during Watergate or the Iranian hostage crisis, when the press plays a principal role in focusing Americans' attention. During Reagan's first term, no lapse in control was ever sustained long enough for the president to suffer serious political damage. Even events such as the devastating bombing of the American soldiers' billet in Beirut or Reagan's visit to Bitburg cemetery in Germany generated controversies that soon dissipated.

No insidious alchemy led to Reagan's success. In brief summary, his principal skills in dealing with the news media were these:

- He understood how to effectively use television to "sell" himself and his policies;
- He avoided as much as possible formats in which he was weak, such as news conferences;
- He had a staff highly skilled in creating media events that worked to his advantage;
- He had an instinctive feel for what Americans wanted to hear, and that is what he told them.
- He cultivated personal popularity to such a degree that it usually protected him not only from attacks by other politicians, but also from press criticism.

Journalists contemplating Reagan's success sometimes wonder if the press has done its job properly. In retrospect, could coverage of the Reagan campaigns and his first term have been tougher and more substantive?

Given the self-imposed rules of coverage, the news media probably could have done little differently. An instinctive reaction from a White House reporter is to say, "We shouldn't cover every photo opportunity that the president's staff dreams up."

That suggestion is fine in principle, but no major news organization is likely to boycott covering the President of the United States because they believe they are being taken advantage of. The chances of something interesting (or tragic) happening while the press is absent is every reporter's nightmare, so the president will continue to be covered whatever he does and however manipulative it seems.

On the other hand, reporters do get lazy. A kind of inertia keeps some correspondents close the White House press room or sitting on the campaign bus, waiting for handouts when they might be able to dig up better stories on their own. Despite the resources at his disposal, neither Reagan nor any other president has a monopoly on information. In covering Reagan, as was the case in the coverage of his predecessors, many reporters could always be more aggressive.

Reagan also benefited from the relative ineptitude of his opponents. Neither Jimmy Carter nor Walter Mondale fully understood the power of television, and neither man was adequately skilled in its use to compete effectively against Reagan. Beyond television, Carter and Mondale also failed to appreciate how the media influence voters' perceptions of their leaders. Political reality dictates some wooing of the press. Reagan did this better than either of his Democratic opponents.

Even when Reagan was not campaigning for votes, he consistently used the news media to outmaneuver his Democratic opponents in Congress. In late 1985, for example, Reagan traveled to Capitol Hill to try to save tax reform legislation. To the nation watching this on their evening newscasts or seeing the headlines in their newspapers, the president was being accommodating in the cause of reform.

This gesture of visiting the Capitol—really another media event—put Reagan's congressional opponents in an untenable position. Once again, Reagan had deftly put public opinion in his pocket.

The politician who lives by television can be undone by television. A good example of this is found in the political difficulties that swamped Reagan during his second term.

For Reagan, 1987 was not a good year. As public concern grew about the sale of arms to Iran and the diversion of the sale's profits to Nicaraguan contras, Reagan's competence as chief executive was called into question. During the summer, much of the country watched the fascinatingly complicated daily soap opera of the congressional hearings during the Iran-contra affair.

As in any good TV series, the cast of characters was varied: Lt. Col. Oliver North, the swashbuckling entrepreneur of covert action; Admiral John Poindexter, the avuncular mastermind with a faulty memory; George Shultz, the maligned hero staging a comeback; Fawn Hall, the glamorous ingenue. At the hearings, these and others told their stories to the television camera and thus to the nation. Their testimony painted a picture of a White House in disarray, presided over by a president so disengaged from important policy and management decisions that power was being wielded by whoever was daring enough to do so.

Reagan tried to rally his waning public support with his own tried and true tactic—a televised speech to the nation. It didn't work. The extensive coverage of the hearings had so undermined the President's position that he was unable to regain his credibility.

Whenever public opinion is important in deciding the outcome of a particular political battle, news coverage affects policy-making. The 1987 Senate Judiciary Committee hearings following President Reagan's nomination of Robert Bork to the Supreme Court offer a case in point.

When the hearings began, most of the committee members had already made up their minds about whether they were going to support the nomination. For those senators who were undecided (both those on the committee and other members of the body), the hearings gave them two kinds of assistance in making their decision.

First, they could watch Bork in action as he discussed his past decisions and judicial philosophy. But second, the senators could gauge how the American people responded to Bork.

It can be argued that the real purpose of the senators on the committee, particularly those who had no doubt about how they eventually would vote, was to use the hearings not primarily as a forum for senate decision-making, but rather as a kind of "trial by television" for Bork. Opponents of Bork, such as Senators Joseph Biden and Edward Kennedy, were often talking through Bork and through their colleagues directly to the mass audience that was watching the hearings. These senators, as well as some supporting Bork, were making their case to the American people, knowing that extensive polling was going on during the hearings and that the results of those polls would influence senators who hadn't yet decided how to vote.

Bork didn't do particularly well in the hearings, at least not in the sense of being able to match the television skills of many of the senators. The polls reflected this and his already wounded nomination was eventually voted down by the full senate.

Yet another media aspect of the Bork nomination was the appearance of competing television commercials sponsored by supporters and opponents of Bork. The anti-Bork spots, one of which was narrated by actor Gregory Peck, seemed to attract the most attention and exacerbated Bork's political predicament.

The Bork episode can be viewed as an example of positive and negative media influence. This certainly was the most public debate about a Supreme Court nomination, and, given the power of that office, democracy probably was well served by such visibility.

On the other hand, perhaps format unduly dictated content, in the sense that complicated matters of legal philosophy and constitutional interpretation often were boiled down to an absurdly simplistic level. Again, Bork was clearly out of his element when debating senators who were so experienced in working in front of the cameras.

Should the ability to perform on television be a criterion for sitting on the Supreme Court? Few people would say yes. But, as Bork's opponents would be quick to argue, a nominee to the highest court should be able to explain his positions on crucial issues to the public. Televised hearings are the best way for that to happen.

At least some of the future nominees to the Supreme Court are also likely to be tested on television. Perhaps the process will eventually settle down to a more thoughtful debate about matters of substance and media coverage will be a more passive factor.

During these few months of 1987, Reagan learned the painful lesson that when a president loses his relatively monopolistic control of the airwaves, he can quickly find himself out-gunned by his opponents. If the Iran-contra scandal and the Bork debate had been covered merely via the regular news vehicles, Reagan might have been able to use television for speeches and perhaps some staged media events to win support for his positions. That had been his technique throughout most of the first years of his presidency.

But the news media—especially television—gave Congress a rare chance to reach the public in a way that is usually given exclusively to the president. The resulting balance between executive and legislative branches worked to Reagan's detriment.

Lessons exist here for presidents and the news media alike. Even a president who relies on his personal popularity as much as Reagan does can find himself in trouble if the news media let the public get a good look at what is going on. News coverage certainly didn't create the Iran-contra scandal or cause Bork's demise, but it did expand the debate to a point at which Reagan was unable to assert his usual dominance. This can be seen as a further democratizing of the way the country is governed. If news organizations were to provide such extensive coverage more consistently, a new parity might stabilize the powers within the government.

Ronald Reagan, our oldest president, turned out to be our most modern in terms of his understanding and use of mass media. Although the Iran-contra scandal destroyed the "teflon" mystique and proved again the news media's power to influence the course of a presidency, Reagan's political career certainly will be studied closely by other politicians eager to duplicate his success, and it should also be closely studied by journalists who appreciate the necessity of maintaining a dynamic tension in the relationship between press and politician.

8 | Political Advertising— An Evolving Craft

News coverage is "free media." Although politicians try to influence the content and tone of news reports, they can do little to actually control the precise look and sound of a news story. Advertising, on the other hand, is "paid media." If the candidate pays to produce a media message and then pays to print, broadcast, or otherwise transmit it, he can pretty much say whatever he wants. And he can say it wherever he wants, in the pages of a newspaper that has given him negative coverage or on the air of a television or radio station that's given him no coverage at all.

Advertising and News

Sometimes denounced as being the worst kind of hucksterism, filled with distortions of the facts, if not outright untruths, political ads, more often than not, do little other than encapsulate the most favorable aspects of a candidate's image or the issues he is stressing.

Advocates of political advertising argue that because news coverage is so dominated by superficial "media events," campaign advertising often presents more insight into a candidate's character and more substantive discussion of issues than news reports do.

This debate will continue indefinitely, but campaign advertising has clearly become an invaluable tool for candidates seeking to redress the balance of the press-politician relationship when they think the news media have achieved too great an advantage.

The sophistication of campaign advertising has increased dramatically in recent years, easily keeping pace with advances in news-gathering technology. State-of-the-art advertising, as is used in presidential campaigns, has proved to be an exceptionally potent tool, although it is used more for strengthening already existing attitudes than for building support from scratch.

An effective campaign ad has a specific message, is aimed at a specific audience, is designed to provoke a specific reaction, and is well enough produced that it will stand out amidst the barrage of advertising to which all Americans are subjected.

Different ads are prepared for different purposes. The variations may be obvious, such as Spanish-language radio spots aimed at Hispanics, or more subtle, such as changing the background of ads depending on each ad's message.

In two television ads run during a 1984 U.S. Senate race, one about aid for public education and the other about Social Security, the candidate sat in an office setting, in front of his desk. In the education spot, a framed photograph on the desk showed the candidate, his wife, and two young children. In the Social Security spot the setting was exactly the same, except the photo in the frame was of two older persons, presumably the candidate's parents.

Concern about such nuance might seem silly, but candidates rely heavily on their ads. Usually, campaign ads don't change voters' minds; rarely will someone who favors Candidate A see an ad for Candidate B and suddenly switch support to B. Rather, the political ad is reinforcement, a nudge to the voter who is already committed, or at least leaning, to one candidate. The ad can strengthen the level of support and make it more likely that the voter will go to the polls on election day.

History of Political Ads

The history of political advertising can be divided into two distinct eras: the years before television and the years since television began giving us "the 30-second president"—the candidate packaged neatly in a TV spot. The first television advertising of consequence appeared during the 1952 presidential race, but 1960 marked the real arrival of television power. By that year, 90 percent of American households had television sets.

Ads Before Broadcasting

Early American political salesmanship makes even the toughest of today's ads seem mild by comparison. Handbills distributed in the John Adams versus Thomas Jefferson presidential contest in 1796 denounced Jefferson as an atheist and Adams as a monarchist.

The 1828 race pitting Andrew Jackson against John Quincy Adams saw handbills, banners, and even "official campaign biography" promoting Jackson's image as "Old Hickory," the heroic soldier.

The Jackson technique was carried further in 1840 by supporters of General William Henry Harrison, the "hero" of a minor battle against Indians at Tippecanoe, Indiana. With Harrison and vice presidential candidate John Tyler, the ticket picked up the slogan "Tippecanoe and Tyler Too." This nice bit of alliteration inspired the first noted campaign song. Harrison also was portrayed as a "log cabin candidate" (although he actually was born in a very comfortable farmhouse), a device that proved so successful, candidates who followed were quick to embrace their real or invented humble beginnings.

Before the twentieth century, most candidates engaged in very little on-the-road campaigning. For example, William McKinley, in 1896, spent much of his time on the front porch of his Canton, Ohio, home waiting for the voters to come to him. William Jennings Bryan was a traditional, crowd-pleasing orator who loved the torchlight parades and other accoutrements of old-time campaigning, but he was defeated each of the three times he was the Democratic nominee.

Radio Arrives

The decline of the stump speech accelerated in the 1920s with the advent of radio. In 1924, there were three million radios in America. By 1934, the number had grown to 30 million, and it kept climbing. This box of wires and tubes meant the candidate's voice no longer had to be contained within the auditorium or fairgrounds where he spoke. Suddenly, the candidate's words could reach millions.

The nature of the candidate's voice also changed. The booming oratory that could carry to the outer reaches of a crowd of several thousand was no longer appropriate. Now the voice could reach millions, but it did so most effectively as conversational, nontraditional speech-making.

Politicians first used radio by simply buying time and talking to as large an audience as pre-network hook-ups could reach. People might listen even to long-winded speeches just for the novelty of hearing sound come over the airwaves. But as time passed and more stations began to broadcast, audiences tended to tune out the politicians in favor of straight entertainment. To spice up candidates' broadcasts, the first forms of political broadcast advertising were born.

Listeners' interest was held by dramatic narrative interspersed with bits of music and endorsements by celebrities. For instance, daytime radio audiences in 1948 heard brief dramatizations produced by the Harry Truman campaign: the "average housewife" complained about rising food prices that she blamed on the Republican Congress.

As listeners became even more discriminating, the length of political broadcasts began to shrink. From the hour-long speeches of the 1930s, we have moved to the 30-second spots of the 1980s. Also, broadcast time has become increasingly expensive, so few campaigns can afford to purchase large chunks of air time.

Radio spots were the logical complement to print advertising, which had evolved from the Adams-Jefferson handbills first into tabloids distributed by the campaign organizations and then into space purchased in newspapers and magazines. Print ads sometimes alerted listeners to the candidate's upcoming radio spots. Voters began to experience the sensory barrage known as "multimedia" advertising.

Television Arrives

Harry Truman and Thomas Dewey both used television to speak to voters in 1948, but this new electronic curiosity was to be found in few American homes then. Not until 1952 did politicians begin to rely on television as a significant element of campaign strategy.

1952: EISENHOWER VERSUS STEVENSON

During this year of the Dwight Eisenhower versus Adlai Stevenson race, Americans were buying television sets. The percentage of households with televisions rose from nine percent in 1950 to 65 percent by 1955. Many politicians had sense enough to ride the crest of this wave.

Republican nominee Eisenhower made good use of TV advertising in this initial year of political spots. However, his Democratic opponent, Stevenson, preferred giving speeches and loudly complained about the compressing force of television.

Eisenhower's television advertising campaign was something of a test tube case, and his ads became the responsibility of one of Madison Avenue's wizards, Rosser Reeves.

By 1952, Reeves was well on his way to making millions by creating television messages to sell products more tangible than political candidacies. Reeves told us M&Ms would "melt in your mouth . . . not in your hand," and he urged us to take Anacin "for fast, fast, fast relief."

Reeves devised a variety of packages in which to wrap Eisenhower. A biographical montage underscored Eisenhower's wartime leadership. A lighter touch was found in an animated "I Like Ike" spot, with art work provided by the Walt Disney studios and music by Irving Berlin.

Most memorable were the "Eisenhower Answers America" spots in which the candidate appeared to be responding to questions put to him by average citizens. Actually, Eisenhower had taped his punchy "answers" without ever seeing his questioners. After the General had done his filming in New York, Reeves needed "typical Americans" to be the questioners. So Reeves went to Radio City Music Hall, and among the tourists visiting there found persons willing to become "stars" on Ike's commercials.

The product of these efforts looks remarkably unsophisticated when compared to today's ads. When these spots aired, however, they helped establish Eisenhower as a candidate with a fresh approach to issues. After 20 years of Democratic control of the White House, this was an important selling point for the GOP nominee.

The Republicans outspent Stevenson and the Democrats by better than two to one for television time. Eisenhower's victory cannot be attributed solely to his television appeals, but certainly the spots helped.

The most noteworthy use of political television in 1952 was not a conventional ad, but was the "Checkers speech" delivered by GOP vice presidential nominee Richard Nixon. Accused of receiving contributions to set up a personal slush fund, Nixon was on the verge of being dropped from the ticket by Eisenhower, who was trying to make Democratic corruption a major issue.

Nixon, with his wife, Pat, sitting dutifully nearby, gave a live, prime-time speech defending himself. He talked about his lack of wealth and his wife's need to wear not mink, but "a good Republican cloth coat." The most memorable line in the speech came when he referred to gifts he had received, including a dog named Checkers that had been given to his two young daughters. Nixon said that come what may, he would not take the dog away from his daughters.

The speech resulted in a wave of sympathy for Nixon. He remained on the ticket and went on to a long career in which television continued to be a major factor.

1956: EISENHOWER VERSUS STEVENSON (ROUND 2)

By 1956, when Stevenson again ran against Eisenhower, the Democrats had recognized they would have to adapt to the demands of television. Even Stevenson, who still disliked what he considered to be the superficiality imposed by TV, agreed to appear in spots designed to make him look less intellectual and more folksy. This effort didn't produce much either in image or votes.

Eishenhower's ads relied on the candidate's personal popularity and the power of incumbency. With a variety of crises underway around the world (revolt in Hungary and fighting in the Middle East, among others), the image of Eisenhower the statesman was added to the image of Eisenhower the general.

The Democrats made a strategic error in 1956 by attacking Eisenhower in some of their spots. Using excerpts from the Republicans' own 1952 "Eisenhower Answers America" spots, the Stevenson campaign accused Eisenhower of not living up to his promises.

Negative advertising of this kind entails a calculated risk. If you convince voters that a supposed paragon really isn't all he pretends to be, you can inflict considerable damage on your opposition. But if this attack is launched against someone voters want to believe and trust, the ads can backfire. That is what happened to the Democrats in 1956.

Not all of Eisenhower's policies were popular, but the old general himself was the nation's father-figure. Ike seemed to be above politics and the Democrats ended up looking like partisan hacks when they tried to defile the image of the President.

Undoubtedly, memories of this unsuccessful foray against Eisenhower played a role in later campaigns' strategizing. In 1984, for example, Mondale generally resisted attacking Reagan himself, aiming his barbs instead at Reagan administration policies. Based on polls showing Reagan's enormous personal popularity, any tactics seen by voters to be chastising the President probably would have hurt Mondale more than their target.

1960: NIXON VERSUS KENNEDY

After Eisenhower rolled to an easy victory in 1956, television power took another quantum leap forward. By the beginning of the 1960 campaign, approximately 90 percent of American households had television sets, thus allowing unprecedented pervasiveness of news, commercial messages, and other programming.

The Kennedy-Nixon campaign of 1960 was a milestone in campaigning not only due to the televised debates between the two men, but also to more sophisticated advertising.

Some of Kennedy's spots had the look of mini-documentaries. While Kennedy talked with coal miners, the camera would not focus exclusively on the candidate, but also on the grime-covered face of one of the miners. Surrounded by a crowd of questioners, Kennedy responded to questions about whether his Catholicism would interfere with his possible presidency. Excerpts included from the debates showed Kennedy delivering forceful, articulate answers while cutaway shots showed a scowling, shifty-eyed Nixon.

These spots had the advantage of not appearing as self-serving as those filmed with the standard studio look. Composition of these ads looked much like the footage viewers were used to seeing on newscasts. This made the spots seem more credible.

Credibility is not easily achieved in any advertising, especially that for political candidates. Voters are skeptical consumers. They are wary of being conned. Voters' cynicism about politicians combined with their skepticism regarding advertising makes them a difficult audience for political ads to affect. That is why many political ads tend to follow the pattern used in the documentary style of some of Kennedy's spots. The "slice of life" approach, even when carefully planned and the result of many hours of filming, seems closer to "reality"; thus its message is more likely to be accepted by voters.

1964: GOLDWATER VERSUS JOHNSON

The most notable political ads of the 1964 campaign, when Kennedy's successor, Lyndon Johnson, was challenged by Republican Barry Goldwater, were tough, negative ads produced by the Democrats and designed to scare the hell out of voters, especially some selected audiences within the overall electorate.

Best-remembered of these spots was the "daisy" commercial. A little girl stands in a field plucking petals off a daisy and counting them in her childish voice. When she reaches "nine," the picture of the girl freezes and an adult male voice begins counting down from ten. The camera moves tight on the freeze frame of the girl, ending up focused on her eye, which is looking pensively upward. When the man reaches "one," the video cuts to an explosion of a nuclear bomb. As the screen fills with a fiery mushroom cloud, Lyndon Johnson's voice tells viewers: "These are the stakes—to make a world in which all God's children can live, or go into the dark. We must love each other, or we must die."

At no time was Barry Goldwater's name mentioned, but, not surprisingly, some viewers thought the commercial was telling them that Goldwater would let little girls be nuked.

The Goldwater campaign screamed "Foul," and the Democrats, with much virtuous protesting that they didn't mean to imply Goldwater was a warmonger, pulled the spot after its single showing.

Even two decades after that spot was produced, it remains a jarring 30 seconds of video. This commercial exemplifies the power of advertising, and some would argue it also demonstrates the fundamental dangerousness of the political spot. By using a shocking, dramatic spot apparently to insinuate an opponent's political position, the advertising strategists were distorting a candidate's views and nonsensically simplifying a complex issue.

Perhaps voters are smart enough to resist such tactics, but this spot unquestionably had impact. At the very least, it kept alive doubts about Goldwater's fitness to deal with issues of war and peace.

Control of nuclear weapons was an important issue in the 1964 campaign, but does this kind of advertising foster reasoned debate about that issue? Should issues and candidates be treated with the same simplistic glibness that might be used to sell detergent?

Goldwater had made himself an inviting target. At one point he had talked about "lobbing one into the men's room of the Kremlin" and had asked for trouble with his own oversimplified approaches to issues ranging from nuclear testing to Social Security.

The Democrats' ads made use of whatever faux pas Goldwater provided. Goldwater once said he thought it wouldn't be a bad idea "to saw off the eastern seaboard and let it float out to sea." In a Johnson spot, an announcer quoted Goldwater while a saw attacked a wooden map of the United States. With a splash, the east coast dropped off. Voters in eastern states presumably got the message.

Goldwater had also raised the possibility of making Social Security funding voluntary, a plan his critics charged would quickly bankrupt the system. A Johnson ad raised this issue, with the announcer noting that even Goldwater's running mate, Congressman William Miller, didn't think this was a good idea. The video displayed a pair of hands going through photos and cards such as would be found in anyone's wallet. After shuffling through to the Social Security card, the hands rip it in half. This ad certainly must have frightened older citizens who depend on Social Security.

One of the nastiest anti-Goldwater spots showed white-robed Ku Klux Klan members burning crosses. The spot quoted a Klan official saying, "In Alabama, we hate niggerism, Catholicism, and Judaism." The announcer quoted this same Klan leader as saying: "I like Barry Goldwater. He needs our help."

Goldwater's campaign undoubtedly attracted support from radically right-wing individuals and groups. But to imply that Goldwater was the Klan's candidate and was sympathetic to the Klan was unfair. This spot might not have convinced any reasonable person that Goldwater was pro-Klan, but it reinforced voters' worries that Goldwater might be too close to extremist groups. Like the "daisy" ad, the Klan spot didn't go quite so far as to make a direct allegation against Goldwater, but it certainly sowed many seeds of doubt that had to work to the Democrats' advantage.

Trying to mount his own attack, Goldwater appeared in spots denouncing crime, pornography, and political corruption, and pledging to "restore to America a dedication to principle and to conscience among its public servants." The tag line for Goldwater's ads was, "In your heart, you know he's right."

Goldwater even trotted out beloved old General Eisenhower to defend the GOP nominee against what Eisenhower called the "tommyrot" of charges of extremism. A California actor named Ronald Reagan presented a televised speech titled "A Time for Choosing" that endorsed Goldwater with even more rhetorical flourish than the candidate himself had been able to muster.

All this was to no avail. Goldwater carried only six states against Johnson.

1968: NIXON VERSUS HUMPHREY

The sharp edge of Johnson's ads seemed mild when compared to the bitterness that permeated the politics of 1968. This certainly was one of the most traumatic years in American history. The Vietnam War was inspiring political upheaval and civil disobedience that precipitated Lyndon Johnson's withdrawal from the presidential race. Martin Luther King was assassinated in April, spurring violent riots in several American cities. In June, presidential candidate Robert Kennedy was assassinated minutes after claiming victory in the crucial California primary. When the Democrats finally convened for their convention in Chicago in August, demonstrators and police clashed in the streets while delegates stumbled towards their nomination of Hubert Humphrey.

These events set the acrimonious tone of the 1968 presidential campaign. Republicans nominated Richard Nixon and Maryland Governor Spiro Agnew to run against Humphrey and Maine Senator

Edmund Muskie. The political picture was made more complex by the third-party candidacy of Alabama Governor George Wallace, whose campaign was widely perceived as playing on racial biases.

Recriminations about Vietnam and pledges to restore "law and order" quickly began to dominate campaign rhetoric. By the time the Democrats left bloody Chicago, Nixon held a commanding lead in the polls.

The Democrats were badly split: followers of Minnesota Senator Eugene McCarthy, who had shared with Robert Kennedy the support of anti-war voters, were at best unenthusiastic about aiding Humphrey. As Nixon pressed his argument for a change of leadership, Humphrey had to pull his party together before making claims he could govern effectively as president.

As in any campaign, the advertising reflected the mood of the country and the general tenor of political debate. One of the toughest Republican spots showed still photos of street riots and bodies in Vietnam intercut with pictures of Humphrey while the song "Hot Time in the Old Town Tonight" played dissonantly in the background. The only words spoken during the spot came from an announcer at the end: "This time, vote like your whole world depended on it. Nixon."

This ad portrayed Humphrey as uncaring and somehow at fault for war and crime. Once again, a TV spot had been used to reduce complex issues to devastatingly simplistic terms.

Another Republican spot played on widespread fear of rising crime rates. In this ad, the video is of a woman walking along a deserted city street at night. An announcer recites crime statistics and concludes: "And it will get worse unless we take the offensive. Freedom from fear is a basic right of every American. We must restore it."

In both these spots, Nixon himself is never seen or heard. A tag line at the end identifies whom the spot is promoting. Nixon's planners knew their candidate was not well loved, so they deemphasized him while stressing their opponent's failings.

Humphrey, in addition to striking back at the Republicans, had to reinforce his own position. He did this partly through ads stressing his accomplishments from the years in the Senate that preceded his becoming vice president. The Humphrey message cited the Job Corps, fair housing and civil rights legislation, aid to education, and other progressive issues.

Through these efforts, Humphrey was trying to reclaim the Democratic "citizenship" that many members of his own party felt he had relinquished by so steadfastly supporting the Johnson administration's Vietnam policy.

Humphrey's true breakthrough in the campaign did not occur until September 30, barely a month before the election. On that day, Humphrey gave a nationally televised speech from Salt Lake City in which he promised, "As President, I would stop the bombing of North Vietnam as an acceptable risk for peace . . . ." This final break with the Johnson war policy gave Humphrey impetus as he entered the homestretch of the campaign.

The bombing halt speech did much to rally previously disgruntled Democrats. Meanwhile, Humphrey's advertising was chipping away at the Nixon lead. The Democrats identified a Republican weakness: vice presidential nominee Spiro Agnew.

Agnew had accused Humphrey of being "squishy soft on communism," a phrase that reminded many listeners of the red-baiting Joe McCarthy. Agnew also had developed a talent for making comments certain to boomerang, such as, "If you've seen one slum, you've seen them all."

Some Democratic ads compared Agnew's credentials to those of his Democratic opponent, Edmund Muskie, whose distinguished record in the Senate dwarfed Agnew's limited accomplishments. A famous Democratic television spot ridiculed Agnew by treating his candidacy as a joke. The video is simple: a shot of a television set. On the screen is lettered, "Agnew for Vice President?" The only audio is a person's wild, uncontrollable laughter. At the end of the spot, while the laughter continues, the video cuts to lettering that reads, "This would be funny if it weren't so serious."

The Republicans claimed this ad was just as unfair as Johnson's "daisy" spot four years before. (Both ads had been produced by the same man, Tony Schwartz.) This criticism was based on the ad's lack of substance: it gave no explanation of Agnew's alleged failings.

Despite these protests, even top Republicans were uneasy about Agnew. As in most national campaigns, the vice presidential candidate was pushed into the background. (Instances such as the Ferraro candidacy in 1984 are the exception, not the rule.)

This was a Nixon campaign, and Nixon was determined to prove he had learned his lesson from his 1960 loss to John Kennedy. No more sweating under television lights; no more nonchalance in preparing for television appearances. The byword for Nixon in 1968 was "control."

Nixon remembered how television had hurt him and helped Kennedy eight years before. By 1968, Nixon realized voters would place a perhaps inordinate amount of trust in what they saw on their TV screens. Nixon's aides knew how to arrange television campaigning so it would retain the appearance of spontaneity while actually being precisely planned.

Republican media planners liked the way Nixon handled himself in front of a panel of "citizens" (i.e., not journalists) who asked questions about a wide range of issues. Selecting this panel involved finding people who "looked right" in the sense of generating a feeling of kinship with members of the television audience. Questioners who might become too prosecutorial if they didn't like Nixon's answers were weeded out.

After several hours of questions and answers were taped, five-minute ads and a half-hour program were assembled from the material. The final versions gave the impression that Nixon was performing in a public forum and facing truly challenging questions. Viewers rarely stopped to think about what they were not seeing or wonder about Nixon's answers that were edited.

The Nixon campaign used these taped ads during the primaries, but during the general election campaign they ventured into live broadcasts, sometimes including journalists on the panel. These programs took place before large and highly partisan studio audiences, screened carefully to ensure sympathetic responses to Nixon's comments.

Nixon used both the taped and live versions of these panel sessions to keep his distance from the press. Reporters were generally excluded from the taping sessions. This angered them because they wanted to be able to report on what the candidate had said even if it didn't end up in the final edited product. Nixon's campaign aides were unmoved by this argument; the press was kept out.

Even in the live broadcasts, reporters were kept away from the studio and confined to a nearby room where they could watch the session on a television set. Nixon's staff maintained this was so reporters could see the event just as people at home saw it.

Reporters complained about having to write about the program without having a first-hand feel for the dynamics of the studio audience or a close look at Nixon under pressure. Again, the Nixon staff was unmoved by such protests.

Critics of the exclusion of the press from the Nixon television campaign got belated revenge. In 1969, a young journalist named Joe McGinniss published a book titled, *The Selling of the President 1968*.

An uncharacteristically generous decision by the Nixon media hierarchy had given McGinniss remarkable access to meetings and documents that were key elements in shaping the 1968 strategy. What emerged was a devastating portrait of hucksterism and manipulation—a campaign managed by bigoted boors who felt no obligation to the public, and who were concerned with winning the election at any price.

McGinniss' narrative and the lengthy documentation he provided are highly entertaining, but his book also served the important purpose of increasing public and press scrutiny of the political advertising business. As part of the coverage of many campaigns today, reporters do stories about the candidates' ads, challenging their accuracy when appropriate, and letting the public see how far Madison Avenue techniques have intruded into the political process.

The news media have taken notice, somewhat belatedly, of the tremendous power inherent in political advertising. Reporters can argue forcefully that the impact ads have on voters justifies press access to the system that generates those ads: no more closed-door productions such as the early Nixon panel shows.

Politicians generally resist this idea. They argue that reporters can critique the ads when they appear, but have no right to demand access to the strategizing and production behind the advertising. This debate continues; it is yet another example of the push-and-pull that goes on between press and politicians.

Nixon's emphasis on control and caution worked no miracles. Despite the Democrats' internal divisions and the huge lead Nixon held at the beginning of the campaign, the Republican ticket barely won the election. Nixon defeated Humphrey by only 500,000 votes out of approximately 73 million cast. Nixon won 43.4 percent of the vote to Humphrey's 42.7, while George Wallace won 13.5 percent (almost 10 million votes).

One reason for Nixon's win was probably his edge in broadcast advertising. The Republicans spent $6.3 million on television time; the Democrats spent $3.5 million. Total broadcast expenses— including production, agency fees, and radio time—cost the Republicans $12.6 million, while the Democrats paid $6.1 million.

1972: NIXON VERSUS MCGOVERN

When Nixon ran for re-election in 1972, he was both frontrunner and incumbent. His presidency was troubled by the continuing war in Vietnam and by early rumblings about a "third-rate burglary" of the Democratic Party headquarters in the Watergate office building, but the Nixon campaign style, and his advertising, reflected cool confidence.

The Democrats once again were in disarray, never having healed fully from their 1968 agonies. The leading advocate of party reform, South Dakota Senator George McGovern, was the nominee.

New legislation placed a ceiling on campaign spending. Nixon and McGovern each were limited to $14 million for post-convention costs, of which only $8.4 million could be spent on broadcasting.

The Republicans' strategy was simple: cloak Nixon in the majesty of the presidency—making him "the President," never "the candidate"—and let surrogates such as Vice President Agnew play the role of "heavy" in attacking the Democrats.

Nixon's ads stressed his accomplishments as world leader by using footage from his visits to the Soviet Union and China. Other spots tried to "humanize" this president for whom few voters felt much real affection. One of these ads showed Nixon at the White House piano leading a chorus of "Happy Birthday" for jazz composer Duke Ellington.

McGovern was perceived as being among the most liberal of Democrats, so Nixon didn't have to worry about holding conservative voters. Few Republicans would defect, and polls showed McGovern unlikely to do well with independents. To turn a victory into a landslide, however, Nixon needed to pull Democrats— particularly Southerners and conservative blue collar workers— away from traditional party loyalties and induce them to cast their ballots based on ideological preference.

This led to creation of "Democrats for Nixon," which sponsored some tough, anti-McGovern ads. Principal spokesman for this group was John Connally, who had served as a Democratic Governor of Texas and as Nixon's Secretary of the Treasury.

A main target of the "Democrats for Nixon" spots was McGovern's proposals for cutting defense spending. In one ad, Connally made this pitch on camera. A more effective spot showed toy soldiers, ships, and planes being swept away by a hand while an announcer described how McGovern's proposal allegedly would cripple America's defenses.

These ads featured the kind of exaggeration common to political campaigns. McGovern had been ineffective in easing fears that he was a liberal extremist, so these spots increased voters' wariness about the Democratic nominee.

McGovern tried to counter-punch with spots focusing on Nixon's failure to end the Vietnam War, which McGovern's ads called "the greatest military, political, economic, and moral blunder in our national history."

A spot McGovern used throughout the primaries and general election campaign showed the candidate talking with a group of disabled young war veterans. An announcer begins, "Most of them were still safe in grade school when this man first spoke out against the war." Much of the spot features conversation between McGovern and the young men, many of whom are in wheelchairs. The veterans discuss their plight and McGovern responds, "I love the United States, but I love it enough [that] I want to see some changes made."

McGovern spots also criticized the Republicans' attempts to sabotage the Democrats' campaign. Details of Watergate were beginning to surface, but the full extent of the scandal was not revealed until after the election. As in the Vietnam spots, McGovern hammered away at the need for the president to be a moral leader.

In retrospect, the McGovern spots are powerful. The casualties of the Vietnam War and the crimes of Watergate would seem reason enough to vote against Nixon. But Nixon was adroit enough to dodge these issues, promising an eventual "honorable peace" in Vietnam (and using his trips to Russia and China as evidence of his negotiating skill) and denying any complicity in the Watergate burglary.

More important, the Nixon campaign was able to divert voters' attention with the ferocity of its own attacks on McGovern. Republican portrayals of McGovern as being dangerously weak were accepted by voters and outweighed their concerns about Nixon.

The Nixon strategy paid off with a massive win. McGovern received only 37.5 percent of the popular vote and carried only Massachusetts and the District of Columbia.

Before the next presidential election, the "third-rate burglary" of the Democratic Party's offices at Watergate turned into the biggest political scandal in American history. Richard Nixon resigned (preceded by his vice president, Spiro Agnew, who had resigned to avoid indictment on corruption charges unrelated to Watergate) and for the first time America had a president who had never been elected in a national campaign at least to the vice presidency.

1976: FORD VERSUS CARTER

While Americans recovered from the trauma of Watergate, their disgust with political wheeling and dealing was at an all-time high. This negative mood did much to set the tone of the 1976 presidential race and the advertising the two candidates used.

President Gerald Ford faced several difficult tasks. He had to escape the stain of Watergate; guilt by association tarnished most Republican candidates. For Ford, this was a particular liability since he had granted a presidential pardon to Nixon.

Ford also had to establish his qualifications as president. Never before had he represented a constituency larger than a single congressional district. He had to prove that his rapid elevation from the House of Representatives to the White House was not more than he could handle.

The initial obstacle Ford had to overcome if he was to retain the presidency was Ronald Reagan, who was mounting a major campaign for the GOP presidential nomination.

Although he had been in office for less than two years, Ford embraced White House imagery as tightly as possible. Television spots showing Ford at work in the Oval Office included narration such as this: "President Ford's steady, calm leadership has helped put the nation back on track. . . . President Ford has trust in America. America has trust in him. Keep him."

As if he was a psychologist working with millions of patients, Ford tried to raise public confidence in the presidency from its post-Watergate depths. Over video of marching Marine bands and what has become a fairly standard patriotic montage (the Statue of Liberty, a flag being raised, etc.), Americans heard the Ford campaign's irrepressibly cheerful theme song: "I'm feeling good about America; I'm feeling good about me!"

Ford barely survived the Republican primaries and captured the nomination at a bitter national convention. Despite the advertising efforts, Ford never fully disassociated his image from that of Nixon, and Ford's own presidential accomplishments were not of the magnitude to win him the depth of allegiance he would need in his fight against well-organized Democratic opposition.

Just as Watergate crippled the GOP, it revitalized the Democratic Party. Democrats could point at the disgraced Nixon and say, "We told you so," without much fear of being contradicted.

Not even Democratic politicians, however, escaped damage from Watergate. They were, after all, politicians, and many Americans apparently thought that the only difference between the Watergate conspirators and other politicos was that some had been caught and others had not.

Leaping into this breach of faith was a skillful politician who portrayed himself as anything but a politician. Jimmy Carter, former Governor of Georgia, promised he would be different. In his ads, he told voters: "I'll never tell a lie. I'll never make a misleading statement."

To an electorate exhausted by years of Watergate-related lies, Carter's message was welcome. Voters wanted to believe they could elect a different kind of president, so they suspended their skepticism long enough for Carter to build momentum.

The skill with which Carter used advertising to sell this message was evident in a radio spot produced for play on southern stations. This ad combined an appeal to anti-Washington sentiment with an even stronger play on the sympathies of southerners who saw themselves in an "us-against-them" relationship with the rest of the country. These are excerpts: "On November 2, the South is being readmitted to the Union. If that sounds strange, maybe a southerner can understand . . . . Only a southerner can understand what it means to be a political whipping boy. But then only a southerner can understand what Jimmy Carter as president can mean . . . . Are you going to let the Washington politicians keep one of our own out of the White House?"

As the campaign progressed, the Carter strategists made a fundamental change in their basic advertising tone. They had established their candidate as something of an iconoclast, a non-politician who would offer respite from scandal and deceit. Carter was seen in his overalls, walking through Georgia fields, listening to folksy homilies from his mother,"Miz Lillian."

This worked well, but as voters neared the time when they had to decide how they would vote, some questions arose: Jimmy Carter might be a truly good man, but is that the best kind of man for the presidency? Gerald Ford might not be so great, but at least he's a known quantity and he seems unlikely to do anything disastrous. Is Carter really presidential material?

To allay such doubts, "Jimmy in blue jeans" spots gave way to "President Jimmy" ads. Instead of Carter on the farm, we saw a tight shot of Carter in a dark suit sitting in front of an American flag, looking like he belonged in the Oval Office.

Part of this shift was subtle. Carter's message changed less than did his "look." This is a good example of how advertising strategy must be kept flexible and responsive to changes in public opinion. Any presidential campaign has public opinion research pouring in daily, tracking voter attitudes. Shaping those attitudes is what advertising is all about, so a candidate's spots must be responsive to the voters' interests of the moment. Advertising and pubic opinion must travel the same route, each gently tugging on the other.

Carter's altered ad message coincided nicely with campaign events. In the televised debate with Ford, Carter more than held his own with the President. The debate performance and the ads combined to enhance Carter's stature as a prospective national and world leader. This was enough to push some undecided voters into the Democrat's camp.

On November 2, Carter's promise of change outweighed Ford's assurances of dependability. Carter edged Ford by slightly fewer than two million votes out of approximately 80 million cast.

Carter soon learned that the problems a president must face resist even the best of intentions. An intractable Congress, economic instability with roots in past presidencies, and wild foreign leaders foiled Carter's attempts to make his administration work as effectively as he had promised it would.

1980: REAGAN VERSUS CARTER

To Americans who still had not forgotten Watergate, new issues such as the oil embargo and the Iran hostage crisis were further evidence that America was in decline. Carter—whether victim of circumstance or victim of his own leadership style—entered his re-election campaign in 1980 as a beleaguered president. His challengers' campaign advertising would make Carter's competence and America's status in the world the centers of voter attention.

Carter's first test came from within his own party in the person of Senator Edward Kennedy. In the 1980 primaries, Kennedy faced a two-fold task: to rehabilitate his own tarnished image while attacking Carter.

One tough Kennedy TV spot (used in the New York primary, which Kennedy won) showed a photo of a grinning Carter while an announcer said: "This man has misled the American public into the worst economic crisis since the Depression. He's broken promises and cost New York a billion dollars a year. In his latest foreign policy blunder, he betrayed Israel at the United Nations." The video then switched to tape of Kennedy shaking hands in a crowd, while the announcer said (in part): "This man has endured personal attacks in order to lead the fight for specific solutions to our problems . . . . Let's join Ted Kennedy in stopping four years of failure."

This spot served several purposes. It hit Carter hard on matters of importance to New York voters: aid to financially troubled New York City and the U.N. issue, which was of great importance to New York's large Jewish population. The ad also portrayed Kennedy not as a political dilettante, but as an aggressive leader.

Another Kennedy spot pursued the same theme. Video showed Carter at bat in a softball game. While the announcer decried Carter's inaction on inflation, the tape showed the ball crossing the plate while Carter took the pitch, not moving the bat from his shoulder.

Carter, meanwhile, followed the traditional approach of the incumbent: he tried to infuse his ads with the mystique of the White House. (For example, video of Carter at the White House with Pope

John Paul II was used often.) At the same time, he knew the "character issue" would work in his favor against Kennedy, who had never fully emerged from the shadows of the fatal automobile accident at Chappaquiddick.

A typical Carter spot showed the President at work in the White House. An announcer says: "His decisions reach out to touch the lives of millions. In the course of any day, he focuses on every vital issue facing the nation." The viewer then sees Carter speaking, with charts about military matters behind him. Carter is saying, "My number one responsibility is to defend this country, to maintain its security."

So far, this spot has let Carter look presidential. As video of the President continues, the announcer subtly raises the difference between Carter, the citizen president, and Kennedy, the professional politician: "It's nothing at all like being alone in a Georgia field driving a tractor for ten hours in the hot sun. Yet no other candidate can match his work experience or his life experience. President Carter. A solid man in a sensitive job."

Despite his victories in several primaries, Kennedy never was able to damage Carter enough to wrest away the nomination. Carter's campaign, featuring spots that at least implicitly criticized Kennedy, kept the Massachusetts senator sufficiently on the defensive so he could never develop momentum behind a strong, positive campaign of his own. After a bitter Democratic National Convention in New York City, Carter emerged as nominee to face a much tougher opponent: Ronald Reagan.

Reagan's career as candidate, detailed in Chapter Seven, always has benefited from skillful use of television, and that certainly was the case in 1980. Coupled with Reagan's impressive television persona, the GOP advertising was effective in addressing the question any non-incumbent presidential candidate faces: Is he fit for the White House?

In any campaign against an incumbent, that officeholder's record is a principal issue. Reagan used this two ways: he directly attacked Carter's performance per se, and he offered his own style and philosophy as a contrast to Carter's.

One Reagan spot offers a good example of this dual approach. The opening video is of a parade of Soviet troops and military hardware in Moscow. The announcer says, in part: "Ronald Reagan spoke out on the danger of the Soviet arms buildup long before it was fashionable . . . . He has a comprehensive program to rebuild our military power." The video then switches to Reagan, who says: "We've learned by now that it isn't weakness that keeps the peace, it's strength. Our foreign policy has been based on the fear of not being liked. Well, it's nice to be liked, but it's more important to be respected.

The spot achieves its purposes. Reagan quickly is established as favoring a strong defense (a position most voters probably already knew). The urgency of Reagan's position is subtly underscored by stressing the need to *rebuild* American military strength.

Then, without mentioning Carter's name, Reagan hits at what the polls were showing to be a key Carter weakness: the perception that he was soft and was allowing America to be pushed around by a tyrant in Iran.

This spot had to be carefully written. Reagan could not afford to exacerbate fears that he was eager to start a war. GOP strategists remembered Barry Goldwater's demise 16 years before. So, Reagan's spot makes no threats, but plays on voters' worries that America might have become dangerously vulnerable.

Reagan's remarkable adroitness in front of a camera was demonstrated during his debate with Carter and in his election eve telecast. During this 30-minute speech, Reagan invoked the memory of his recently deceased Hollywood friend John Wayne: "To millions he was a symbol of our country itself. Duke Wayne did not believe our country was ready for the dustbin of history. Just before his death, he said in his own blunt way, 'Just give the American people a good cause, and there's nothing they can't lick.'"

When that passage is read some time after it was broadcast, it seems awfully hokey. But Reagan pulled if off. Not even the cynical press corps took him to task for relying on John Wayne to provide the philosophical peroration for the campaign.

Carter's aides were also not oblivious to the help Hollywood could provide. They recruited actor Henry Fonda to host Carter's 20-minute election eve program. The broadcast used some taped segments featuring words of praise for Carter from Edward Kennedy and others and a closing speech by Carter.

Both the rhetoric and delivery were flat, particularly when compared to Reagan's presentation. One of the reasons for this was some sloppy planning by the Carter campaign staff. The only time they could find on the President's schedule for this taping was a few hours after the debate with Reagan.

So, at 5:00 A.M., when Carter certainly was feeling low following his face-off with Reagan, the President sat in a Cleveland hotel room and delivered this crucial speech in one take from the Teleprompter. Carter aides had brought to the hotel room curtains, props, and lighting to give it something of the atmosphere of the Oval Office. This patchwork approach, however, was not the kind of effort that should have gone into such an important broadcast.

On the day following the candidates' final appeals, voters changed presidents. Carter carried only six states and the District of Columbia. Reagan received 51.6 percent of the vote to Carter's 41.7 percent. Independent candidate John Anderson received 6.7 percent.

1984: REAGAN VERSUS MONDALE

After using television effectively throughout his first term as president, Ronald Reagan roared into the 1984 campaign with every intention of winning a sweeping mandate from the American electorate.

The Reagan television advertising in 1984 can only be described as superb, both technically and in its political effectiveness. The spots were exceptionally well produced, with attractive video and low-key music and narration. The candidate's message was delivered equally well, taking credit for a wide range of accomplishments and implicitly claiming that Reagan had restored the presidency and the country to the lofty positions they deserved.

The Reagan ads met a standard many political spots fail to achieve: the production values were comparable to those of product commercials that fill so much of daily broadcast time. This is important for an audience that has become accustomed to high quality video in commercial spots. In fact, some television ads are more attractive and more clever than the regular programming.

When a political spot airs that is not of the same caliber of non-political advertising, viewers are likely to "tune out" and the candidate's message is wasted.

Reagan's 1984 spots were developed not by political communications experts, but by The November Group, a specially assembled team of advertising executives. The same persons who had been encouraging consumers to buy Pepsi Cola were now selling a president.

Several of the Reagan spots began with soft music, a sunrise, and a narrator saying, "It's morning again in America." In a number of these spots, Reagan is not mentioned in the narration, which talks about the availability of jobs, affordability of homes and cars, the lowered inflation rate, and other bullish news.

While this litany proceeds, the video shows viewers an idyllic America: freshly painted houses, clean lawns, not-too-crowded streets, shiny cars (all American-made, of course), a wedding, factory workers arriving at their plant, a fireman raising a flag, a parade down Main Street, and other images designed to make the viewer want to be part of that blissful world. As the flag waves, the narrator reminds the audience that "life is better, America's back," and "Why would anyone want to go back to the way things were four years ago?" Only at the end of the spot is a small picture of Reagan seen.

Late in the campaign, these spots were re-edited, with Reagan himself doing the narration and with a closing segment using an excerpt from Reagan's acceptance speech at the August Republican National Convention.

Other spots used what might be called "travelogue video": aerial photography of the Grand Canyon, Midwest farmland, urban skyscrapers, and the like. The message was similar to the "American town" spots: things are better than ever and "no longer is anyone saying that the presidency is too big a job for any one person."

All these spots offered a mixture of fluff and substance. The ads presented a Norman Rockwell version of America that had a lulling effect: who could ask for a happier, more secure way of life? Behind these images was the narration, gently making Reagan's political case by attributing the idyll to the administration's claimed economic achievements.

The use of the flag in these spots expanded the ads' appeal from one of self-interest to national interest. Reagan consistently has derived political benefit from appealing to patriotism. "America's back" implies that America had gone away. Read between the lines and you get winning in Grenada as a replacement for losing in Iran.

Reagan's strategists knew they could profit from raising the specter of Jimmy Carter. By tying Mondale, who had been Carter's vice president, to unpleasant memories of that administration, the Republicans put their Democratic opponents on the defensive.

Mondale's spots targeted the issues on which Reagan was thought to be most vulnerable: his lack of concern for "ordinary people," and his zeal to expand the arms race. The concept behind the Mondale ads made sense. They showed old people worrying that they would lose Social Security benefits and children who were being shortchanged in their education. Animators created laser-firing satellites that supposedly illustrated the dangers of Reagan's "star wars" plan.

The ideas behind these spots might have been sound, but the execution was weak. Compared to the slick Reagan spots, Mondale's ads looked like relics of earlier campaigns. One spot used the Crosby, Stills and Nash song, "Teach Your Children," which had been popular in the late 1960s, as the audio for a montage of children playing and missiles blasting off. The patchwork look of the spot overwhelmed the message it was trying to convey.

Other than the scare Reagan gave his supporters by his lackluster performance in his first debate with Mondale, the Republican campaign was virtually flawless. Most GOP strategists weren't worried about winning, but only about the size of their margin. Reagan proved their confidence was deserved; he won every electoral vote except the ten from Mondale's home state, Minnesota, and the three from the District of Columbia.

In a campaign such as Reagan's 1984 effort, when the outcome is fairly predictable, advertising performs a different task than it would in a close race. Reagan didn't need to mount a harsh attack on Mondale, so the negative tone in Reagan spots was minimal. (The Republicans did produce, however, some tough anti-Mondale spots to have on hand just in case the race tightened. They were never broadcast.)

Nor was it necessary to "sell" Reagan as had been done in 1980. Polling showed that voters knew Reagan and a substantial majority liked him, even if they didn't approve of each of his policies. The campaign advertising, therefore, was used as reinforcement aimed at making likely Reagan voters certain Reagan voters. This kind of advertising relies on subtle appeal rather than hard sell; it nudges rather than shoves.

The 1984 Reagan television spots set the standard by which the next round of campaign ads will be measured. The Reagan campaign's emphasis on producing "good advertising," not merely "good political advertising," formalized, once and for all, the marriage between advertising and politics.

9 | Political Advertising— Strategies and Techniques

The history of political advertising is one of adaptation. As the technologies of mass media have changed, the art of campaigning has evolved to keep pace.

What Makes an Effective Ad?

Defining "good" political advertising involves varied criteria. The purpose of these ads is to affect voting behavior; that is the ultimate test. Elements that determine this include the following:

• The ad's appearance. Is it striking enough to attract and hold attention? Does it measure up to standards set by the best non-political ads?

• The ad's message. Is the candidate's appeal presented so it can be easily understood by its target audience? Are appropriate issues and themes stressed?

• The ad's penetration. Is the ad presented often enough? Does it use the form of media that will best reach the desired audience?

Truly effective political advertising passes all of these tests. Such ads are the ones voters will remember and politicians will use as models for future campaigns.

Political advertising is different from other ads in a crucial way: the voter must select the candidate by casting a ballot on a particular day. From an advertising standpoint, a political campaign culminates in a "one-day sale."

If the product is soap, not a candidate, the advertising audience—the consumer—may respond at its leisure to the ad message. A political ad must stimulate its audience within a certain 12 hours on election day.

The key to creating successful advertising—political or not—is comprehensive survey research. Before the ads are developed, strategists must decide what the spots will stress. In political advertising, polling not only helps determine a candidate's strengths and weaknesses, but it also probes voters' perceptions of how those strengths can be enhanced and weaknesses remedied.

An advertising planner must know what people will react to. Polling finds out what is in the voter's mind, what feelings the ad can appeal to.

When the 1964 "daisy ad" was created for the Lyndon Johnson campaign, the spot was designed to play on fears about nuclear war. Polling had indicated these fears existed and were working against Barry Goldwater because of what was perceived to be his fast and loose approach to the use of nuclear weapons. By reinforcing those fears, this spot worked to Johnson's advantage.

Similarly, Republican polling in 1984 found lingering negative feelings about the Carter administration. Reagan spots therefore included a few lines reminding voters of how things were during that administration and inviting them to compare Reagan to Carter. All this could be done briefly and subtly because, as the polling had discovered, the feelings were already there and only needed a slight stimulus to work in Reagan's favor.

With survey data in hand, campaign planners must decide what they want their advertising to do for them. Relatively unknown candidates might need to increase their name recognition, so their advertising will be designed to inscribe a name on voters' memories. Other advertising might be used to recite a candidate's qualifications or to explain the candidate's stand on certain issues. Depending on what the polling reveals, any or all of these matters may be the basis for ads.

Much like a campaign speech or a news report, advertising provides a mode of communicating with the public. An advertisement is a message that must be articulated in a way that appeals to both the conscious and subconscious feelings of the voter. The surface of the ad, at first glance, does not always reveal the substance of the message.

A television spot used by Robert Kennedy during the 1968 Democratic primaries is a good example of an ad with several layers of meaning. The spot looks deceptively simple: Kennedy roughhousing on his lawn with several of his children. The music is soft; the conversation between father and children is light-hearted. The brief narration points out that Kennedy, with ten children of his own, can be assumed to be a compassionate politician, concerned about our children's future.

That seems simple enough. But the ad serves several purposes. First, it takes some of the edge off Kennedy's reputation as being cold-blooded. This image had its roots in Kennedy's service as a political "hit man" for his brother and as an aggressive Attorney General. By showing this softer Bobby Kennedy, the spot could remove some of the voters' doubts about the candidate's personality.

The more subtle effect of the spot is its impact on parents who were dreading the prospect of their sons being sent to Vietnam. During 1968, American casualties were rising and the war looked like it would continue for a long time. So even parents with very young sons had to be thinking about finding a way out of the war, a position to which Kennedy was committed. This ad, with its message about the interests of children, was a subtle but effective way to make an anti-war position seem more personal than political.

Historical context is crucial in creating advertising. Voters' decision-making does not take place in a vacuum. They remember past candidates and campaign promises, and they base allegiances on their hopes and fears concerning the present and the future.

Just two years before Johnson's 1964 "daisy" ad appeared, the United States and the Soviet Union came dangerously close to war during the Cuban missile crisis of October, 1962. In 1963, President Kennedy had signed a limited nuclear test ban treaty, which was one of the few signs of hope that the horrors of nuclear war might be prevented. Voters seeing the frightening message of the Johnson spot weren't reacting just to the images on their television screens; their reactions were made stronger by impressions left by these earlier events.

This kind of impact is particularly acute with television spots. Viewers react quickly to what they see on the screen; their response is emotional. After 30 seconds, the ad is gone and programming resumes. Re-reading and pondering the message of a TV ad is impossible. A viewer might remember specifically what he saw, but more likely he will remember the emotion he felt.

Predicting reactions to advertising is a major challenge for campaign strategists. No infallible process exists, but survey data can provide some good bases for such predictions.

In a two-candidate race, the voter actually has four choices. The voter can cast his ballot for or against either candidate. When campaign planners think they know which option voters are most likely to choose, advertising can be tailored to encourage or try to change that course of action.

For example, compare the 1984 Reagan-Mondale race with the 1972 Nixon-McGovern race. In 1984, Reagan aides believed their candidate was well liked and voters would be most likely to vote *for* him, rather than *against* Mondale. Democratic strategists also recognized Reagan's strength and so put much of their effort into winning votes *for* Mondale rather than *against* Reagan. They seemed to concentrate on promoting Mondale and not risking ads that voters might construe as being personal attacks on Reagan.

In any campaign, strategists seek to find the path of least resistance to the voter and then develop the tactics best suited for that path. Once polling helps develop the voter-choice matrix, advertising can be planned to stimulate the appropriate voter sentiments.

This decision has to be made carefully. A misstep could prove damaging, as Adlai Stevenson campaigners discovered in 1956 when they attacked the popular President Dwight Eisenhower.

Also, some pride might have to be swallowed when shaping advertising strategy, as was the case with the 1972 Nixon Campaign. Although Nixon was the incumbent president and heavily favored to win, pragmatic campaigning required GOP planners to spend much of their time launching attacks on McGovern rather than trying to make voters fall in love with Nixon.

This sometimes painful realism must take precedence over "art" in advertising. Everyone has seen snappy commercials for products and remembered jingles or slogans even if not immediately using the products. In politics, however, the imperatives of the "one-day sale" dictate advertising content. If the ad doesn't stimulate a favorable voting decision, it simply isn't a good ad.

An ad's chances of being memorable are increased if rules of good advertising and good politics are followed jointly. For example, the setting of a television spot should be related to the content of the message. A congressional candidate talking about the need for a strong defense probably shouldn't deliver his message while standing in a park or rural setting. Finding a military base isn't hard; a little ingenuity can provide the candidate with a background of rumbling tanks or streaking jets.

Also, the text of an ad should be based on a realistic appraisal of the political sophistication of the audience. For instance, if the candidate wants to talk about inflation, he can do so in brilliant scholarly terms, but virtually no one will understand him. The more logical approach is something like, "I have a young family myself, and I see every week what inflation is doing to the price of groceries and other essential things we need."

That might not be great theoretical economics, but it gets the point across and helps the voter identify with the candidate. That is the kind of ad most likely to be remembered.

One of the most frequently encountered traps in political advertising is the pressure to condense ideas to fit the ad format. Granted, saying much of substance about economic policy in 30 seconds isn't easy, but filling that time with bland generalities produces a worthless ad. It won't have much immediate impact on its audience and it will probably be forgotten quickly.

Far better is taking one aspect of a broad issue and saying something substantive about it. For example, if crime is the issue the candidate wants to address, it makes little sense to use 30 seconds to say crime is bad. If, however, the candidate makes a forceful case for a specific measure, such as mandatory extra sentences for persons using firearms while committing a crime, that clearly stated proposal might catch the attention of the audience.

Voters aren't fools. Over the years, they have heard enough platitudes from candidates, so they know when to tune out a political spot if it isn't saying anything.

Another mistake candidates make is giving an opponent free exposure. If the opponent is mentioned, it should only be in the context of a hard-hitting attack. Stating the opponent's position on an issue and then trying to explain why it is wrong might leave voters pondering the opponent's stance and deciding it isn't so bad after all.

Despite the invaluable aid that survey research provides, creating an advertising message is an imprecise science. All political ads' success or failure is determined largely by the overall context of the campaign. Unforeseen events can cripple a frontrunner or resuscitate a dark horse, and they can make the most cleverly designed advertising strategy instantly obsolete.

Because of the unpredictability of politics, a campaign's advertising plan must be kept as flexible as possible. Using the entire ad budget to produce spots in June for a November election might seem to be great advance planning, but if events of the campaign require a change in strategy (such as responding to an opponent's attacks), the campaign may find itself delivering obsolete ad messages because it has no money to produce new ones.

Ads Using Other Media

Despite the increasing reliance on television as the principal political advertising medium, a well-planned campaign will take advantage of additional ways to deliver its paid messages.

Television has problems born of its power. Advertising on television is enormously expensive. A national 30-second slot on a prime time show with high ratings can cost almost $300,000. Production costs are also high.

Presidential candidates must bear this burden, but local candidates often find television advertising beyond their budgets, particularly since an advertiser must pay at a rate determined by the television station's reach.

For example, a congressional candidate in Dallas, Texas, might care only about reaching that part of Dallas County within his district. If he wants to run television spots, however, he must pay to reach not only other parts of Dallas, but also Fort Worth, Texas (30 miles away), and other cities the Dallas stations reach. Through his spending, the candidate might be convincing lots of people that he is a fine fellow, but a relatively small percentage of this audience will actually be able to vote in his race. (In some communities, cable television allows more precise geographical targeting of audiences.)

Cost-benefit analysis of these kinds of issues deters many candidates from using television. Radio has some advantages that make it preferable to television, particularly in local races.

As with television, radio advertising rates are based on the overall reach of the station, so once again a local candidate will be paying to make his case to an audience that includes many people who can't vote for him. But costs of radio ads—both airtime and production— are far lower than those of television, so the cost-benefit ratio is unlikely to become as lopsided as it might be when running TV spots.

Radio offers relatively precise audience targeting. Most radio stations maintain a consistent format: rock, country, classical, all-talk, or some other dominant theme that attracts its audience. Radio spots can be created with specialized appeals to these different audiences. For example: Spanish-language spots for Hispanic stations, a statement of the candidate's position on arts funding for the classical station, spots oriented to young voters for the rock station, and so on.

Television can offer a less precise version of this specialization. Different audiences watch football games, soap operas, situation comedies, and other programming. The audience research conducted by television networks and individual stations can identify who is watching what, but a television channel's audience tends to be more heterogeneous than that of a radio station.

The relatively lower cost of radio advertising also makes it easier to produce quality spots and saturate the airwaves with ads, particularly during the closing days of a campaign.

Effective radio ads require as much creativity as do television spots. Many people only give a portion of their attention to their radio-listening, so an undistinguished political ad might never register with its audience. The spot needs something (such as distinctive sound effects) to make it stand out from the wave of sound that washes over radio listeners.

Advantages as well as constraints of electronic advertising vanish when a campaign prepares its print ads. The dramatic impact of broadcast spots might be lacking in a newspaper or magazine ad, but the print format allows the candidate to present more information and the voter to read (and perhaps re-read) the material when he wants to, not at an instant dictated by a broadcast schedule.

Different sections of a newspaper attract different kinds of readers, so ads can be geared to these varied audiences. For example, an ad to be placed in the business section might stress the candidate's economic policies, while an ad in the entertainment section might stress the candidate's position on aid to arts institutions.

Print ads also can be used in efforts to offset unfavorable news coverage. Even if a newspaper editorializes against a candidate, it probably will sell ad space to that politician. This gives the candidate an opportunity to state his own case in the same forum in which he was attacked.

As with other advertising media, print demands creative use of the ad space to attract readers' attention. Just as radio generates a solid block of sound from which a spot must stand out, so a newspaper presents a substantial amount of newsprint—much of it ads—from which the politician's message must emerge.

Also like radio spots, print ads are considerably less expensive than television time. Small ads can be sprinkled throughout a day's newspaper at reasonable cost and even full-page ads are not as expensive as most 30-second TV slots.

Many political campaigns make extensive use of outdoor advertising such as billboards, yard signs, and bus backs. Because this kind of advertising seems so unsophisticated, it tends to be underrated. But because it lends itself to simple messages, outdoor advertising is particularly helpful to candidates who need to increase their name recognition. The lower on the ballot a race is, the less attention is generally paid to it. Many people don't vote in every race; they cast their ballots for president, governor, congressman, and a few other high-profile candidates and then leave the voting booth.

Of those voters who remain to decide among the local judicial candidates and others lower on the ballot, not all know very much about these races. Voter psychology—particularly during those few minutes in the voting booth—remains a mystery campaign managers ponder endlessly. Sometimes merely seeing a recognizable name is the stimulus that generates a vote.

That might not say much for the integrity of the democratic process, but it is a fact of life that politicians recognize. Therefore, a candidate knows he might benefit considerably from simply making his name familiar. A large billboard by a heavily traveled expressway provides relatively inexpensive exposure for candidates whose campaign budgets are unlikely to allow television advertising and who probably will attract only cursory news coverage.

The most common form of outdoor advertising is the bumper sticker, which is like a moving, miniature billboard. For a small production expense, a candidate can use his bumper stickers to have his name seen in many places. This isn't a systematic way of reaching voters, but on a limited budget in a campaign that is not attracting much notice, the bumper sticker might spark some initial interest in a candidate that could prove valuable in the voting booth.

Enough visibility of this kind can generate a small bandwagon effect. A person who sees a "Jones for Judge" bumper sticker might ask someone else about the race, and then that person might have his interest aroused, and so on. Again, not too much reliance should be placed on this, but every little bit helps.

The basic rule for outdoor advertising is this: Keep it simple. A billboard crowded with words cannot be read by a driver unless he is in a traffic jam or wants to risk an accident. Outdoor ads are reminders, not convincers. As such, they can be valuable, but they cannot be expected to have profound political effect by themselves.

Campaign advertising takes many other forms. Often these are more expensive than their impact justifies. Campaign buttons have been used for more than a hundred years, but their rising cost has made them less common. Balloons, T-shirts, and coffee mugs have replaced the cigars and whiskey jugs that used to bear the candidate's name and slogan.

These devices probably neither win nor lose many votes. Their danger lies in a campaigner becoming so enamored of such gimmickry that funds needed for more mundane uses are diverted.

More substantive advertising sometimes can be seen in campaign literature. Some of this amounts to nothing more than a slick printing job that conveys no more information than the most superficial TV spot. Other campaign brochures, however, offer good, concise explanations of candidates' positions. In major campaigns it is not unusual to see different brochures prepared to address different issues or to be distributed to different audiences.

Planning Campaign Media

An expensive television spot and a low-budget brochure are designed with a common purpose in mind: To reach a targeted voter with a message carefully designed to stimulate a certain kind of voting behavior. Some ads instill hope, others cause fear. Some inspire a vote in favor of a candidate, others provoke a vote against his opponent.

Success or failure of political advertising is measured by how close the actual voter reaction comes to the reaction that was expected by campaign planners. A long, tortuous path winds from drafting the survey research questions to designing the message and then continuing to the voting booth.

Content is not the only concern of the persons responsible for campaign advertising. Voters' responsiveness to campaigning varies according to a vaguely defined calendar. The old maxim was that the public never paid attention to politics until baseball's World Series was over. That theory was born when baseball was more popular and its season shorter. When the Series ended, a month of campaigning remained.

Today, presidential candidates begin running years before election day; the campaign season seems to have no beginning or end. Political junkies might enjoy this incessant activity, but most people pay only sporadic attention to political campaigns, focusing most intensely during the closing days of the campaign.

To avoid wasting expensive advertising efforts, the campaign must try to synchronize its self-promotion with the unwritten voters' timetable. Pacing is essential, because few campaigns have the money and few voters the interest to sustain a perpetual campaign.

The earliest days of campaigning are times for relying on free media. A candidate's speech might attract some news coverage. Supporters can write to newspapers' "Letters to the Editor" columns commenting on the candidacy. In most campaigns, early advertising should emphasize name identification. If you're like most voters, you won't make an early commitment, but you might take notice that the candidacy is under way.

As the weeks pass, news coverage, and thus your attention, will increase. Advertising then can become more complex, introducing you to a key issue or theme. Just as the candidate at this time will be building an organizational base for his campaign, so too should he be building a base in voters' minds. This will increase his chances of capturing and retaining attention as the campaign proceeds.

Campaign planners at this stage must be careful not to over-reach. Voters will absorb only so much information; barraging them too early with information is a waste of effort and money.

The closer election day draws, the more news coverage and public attention will focus on politics. After several months of campaigning have passed, the candidate can make several assumptions (which can be tested through survey research): name recognition is increasing; voters are finding some issues in which they are interested; the delineation between candidates' views is becoming more clear; and people are making at least tentative decisions about whom they will support.

If the campaigner and you, the voter, are on the same wavelength, the intensity of the vote-seeking effort will increase at the same time you begin seriously considering what you will do on election day. Advertising now can proceed on the assumption that the persons most likely to vote are paying attention and are leaning towards voting a certain way.

A basic rule of politics is to play to strength: First, make certain *your* voters get to the polls, and then try to attract the undecided voters. Leave the opposition's supporters alone; converts are rarely made. The best thing that can happen is for these people to forget about the election.

This rule is most important during the three or four days prior to voting. Countless candidates have lost close elections because the opposition did the best job of getting voters to the polls.

This fear plagues even candidates who hold apparently safe leads. For example, in 1964, Lyndon Johnson's ads ended with the message, "The stakes are too high for you to stay home."

Ads broadcast and printed during the final days are stimuli to encourage people to go to the polls. Television and radio spots should continue during election day, until the polls close. They are not designed to win votes by themselves. That work can only be

accomplished over a long period. This is why the advertising schedule deserves such careful attention from campaign planners.

Impact on Voters

Advertising is invaluable in political campaigns. That is beyond
dispute. The effects of this advertising and questions about
whether it aids or weakens the political process continue to be
debated.

Campaigning today takes place in the living rooms of the voters.
Candidates appear in the home via news reports, their campaign
literature, and various kinds of advertising. Sometimes a journalist
serves as interlocutor, but often the politicians have total control of
the message the voter receives.

Many politicians will argue that advertising improves the caliber
of campaign debate by offering voters needed information that the
news media do not always provide. Critics of this argument charge
that advertising trivializes political debate, reducing complex issues
to slogans and relying on voters' emotions, not their intellects.

This debate will continue forever. While it proceeds, however,
political advertising deserves continuing scrutiny. The power of
these ads is too great to ignore.

The most likely watchdogs are the news media. The process of
selling a candidate through advertising deserves news coverage.
Are the people who appear on a TV spot praising a candidate really
the "average citizens" the ad at least implies they are, or are they
well-rehearsed actors? Is the content of an ad accurate and fair, or
does it distort the facts?

An ever-present fear in campaigns is that some unscrupulous
candidate will barrage voters with false, last-minute advertising,
timed so his opponent will not be able to respond effectively. To
block this, some media organizations refuse to run new ads (those
that have not already been seen publicly before) during the last 48
hours of the campaign. This is designed to ensure time for rebuttal
by a victimized candidate.

Beyond that kind of safeguard, regulation probably is unfeasible
and undesirable. Advertising is a form of political debate and fundamentally is constitutionally protected free speech. Therefore, the

integrity of political advertising depends principally on the good faith of the politicians who create it.

The sophistication of survey research and advertising technique is so advanced that politicians face the temptation to use these skills to manipulate public opinion. Advertising professionals plan the reactions of their audience. For example, campaign strategists know they will generate fear when they create a spot such as Johnson's "daisy" ad, and they expect that fear to affect voting behavior.

Different voters react differently to political ads. Some people probably saw the "daisy" spot and resolved that they would vote for Johnson because Goldwater was dangerous. Other persons seeing the same ad probably thought it was a low blow by Johnson and decided to vote for Goldwater as the candidate with the most integrity.

That lack of a uniform response keeps politicians guessing and tends to keep the system relatively honest. Polling gives politicians a good idea of voters' attitudes, but some unpredictability (of events as well as of public opinion) always has to be added to political equations. Politics remains an inexact science.

10 The Delicate Balance: Status and Prognosis

During a news conference on the day after his defeat at the hands of Ronald Reagan, Walter Mondale was asked what advice he would offer fellow Democrats.

His answer: "I think that, more than I was able to do, modern politics today requires a mastery of television. I think you know I've never really warmed up to television, and in fairness to television, it's never really warmed up to me . . . . I don't think it's possible anymore to run for president without the capacity to build confidence and communications every night."

Mondale wasn't blaming television for his defeat, nor was he claiming he could have won the election had he been more adept in his television appearances. He was, however, acknowledging the dominant role television, and by extension all news media, play in American politics.

These observations offered nothing that many other politicians hadn't already recognized, but the tone of resignation with which Mondale admitted his inadequacy reinforced the notion that candidacies may be subservient to the demands of mass communications media.

Mondale's epitaph for his campaign was a terse summary of the balance, or perhaps imbalance, existing today between the media and politicians. In the continuing tug-of-war for the prize of political power, the media may have greater strength, but is tempered by the presence of candidates such as Ronald Reagan who are exceptionally skilled at taking advantage of media's pervasiveness.

The 1984 presidential race offered examples useful in evaluating the press-politician balance. The news media's clout was demonstrated in the early days of the campaign when the "screening process" helped shape the Democratic field. In what has become a quadrennial ritual, candidates not receiving substantial coverage blamed the news media for their failures in vote-seeking.

Most of these politicians are kidding themselves if they think they would be occupying the White House if only they had received more air time or found themselves on page one more often. Campaign success or failure cannot be ascribed to a single factor.

Their complaints, however, merit attention if only because the news media are so quick to dismiss such protests as sour grapes. Voting behavior *is* affected by news coverage. The John Glenns of the political world are more likely to see their candidacies fizzle if coverage of their campaigns is too harsh or too infrequent. During 1984, Gary Hart proved the press is not omniscient and forced coverage, belated as it was, of his campaign through solid organizational work and an appeal to voters that reporters underestimated. (Hart also benefited from the shortage of strong opponents within his party.)

Whatever the dynamics of a particular campaign year might be, this screening function does much to define voters' options. The role is one the news media have no choice but to assume. Budgets of time, energy, and money demand limits be placed on coverage. Journalists should, however, more thoroughly appreciate the power they wield and use it with the responsibility its effect demands.

As with the screening process, the adversarial relationship between press and politicians was sharpened in 1984. Some aspects of this can be classified as inconsequential competitiveness, such as politicians scheduling pointless media events and reporters resisting these and demanding more substance.

On occasion, however, the competition becomes frenzied. The press' pursuit of Geraldine Ferraro in 1984 at times seemed less a case of investigative reporting than a holy war conducted by journalistic crusaders against political infidels.

Neither reporters nor politicians have yet found a consistent basis for their relationship. They should not be pals, but they shouldn't be mortal enemies. The issue is not one of maintaining decorum; that matters little. But public faith in the political system is fragile and can be shattered if political discourse consists only of invective.

The "us against them" mentality often adopted by both parties to this relationship threatens to turn the efforts of vote seekers and information gatherers into competition for competition's sake.

Who is winning this competition depends on who is judging it. Candidates' reliance on news coverage might indicate that the press has the upper hand, but Ronald Reagan's imperturbable way of carrying the press along in his wake showed that the news media are not always in control.

All political coverage, particularly when news reports are critical of politicians, should be founded on extensive knowledge about politics, ranging from understanding rudimentary political theory to being able to evaluate ingredients of a campaign. The press continues to fall short on these matters. Aside from a few journalists who have had experience working in campaigns, many reporters seem to think that remaining detached means they don't have to know much about what they're covering. This approach increases the likelihood of their being manipulated by clever pols and virtually ensures that coverage will not be as complete as it might be.

This issue is important; the public increasingly depends on the news media as the principal source of political information. News reports, particularly via television, are the windows through which voters watch politicians in action. Candidates, recognizing this, shape their campaigns to meet demands of media.

Whether through false modesty or an inadequate understanding of how powerful they are, the news media don't always recognize how great their responsibilities are as the linchpins of the electoral process. No candidate (with the possible occasional exception of an incumbent president) can reach the voters as consistently and with as much credibility as the news media can.

That should concern journalists, making them impose more stringent tests on their own fairness and accuracy. Nonchalance is a luxury that becomes unaffordable as power increases.

The 1984 campaign offered examples of how a news item can have a life of its own after being removed from the context of its original occurrence. Reagan's stumbling in his first debate with Mondale seemed much more severe when those moments were isolated from the rest of the debate as clips in news stories.

When enhanced through this separation, such events can spawn additional news. Reports saying Reagan would be hurt and Mondale would be helped by the debate created a self-fulfilling prophecy. This was strengthened by follow-up stories that supported the initial premise. People seeing these reports thought Mondale deserved another look, and when they turned out to see Mondale give a speech or march in a parade, they became part of the "growing crowds" news coverage in turn highlighted.

This continued for a few days, but so much time remained before election day that momentum couldn't be sustained. The bubble soon burst and Mondale's campaign didn't benefit much from this journalistic adrenalin.

This example, however, demonstrates the inherent ability the news media have to focus attention on whatever they believe important. Such focusing automatically increases the event's significance, with predictable aftereffects. This is yet another example of press power that can influence election outcomes and therefore should be exercised with exceptional care.

The 1984 Reagan campaign—encompassing the President's personal style, his political strategy, and his advertising—demonstrated that the news media haven't taken full control of the election process.

Reagan's mastery is hard to define, though part of it stems from his unfailing self-confidence. Even when his plan to visit Germany's Bitburg cemetery (where Nazi soldiers are buried) caused great controversy, which was fueled by persistent news stories, Reagan proceeded with his plans and ignored the furor. Of course, he had other concurrent events, such as his visit to Normandy to commemorate D-Day, that overshadowed the Bitburg trip, but basically Reagan didn't allow news coverage to divert his intentions.

Similarly, when Reagan was criticized for his performance in the first debate, he simply plodded ahead with his campaign and White House business, knowing that when the press covered him back on his own turf, the bad images of the debate would blur in the voters' minds.

Reagan and his campaign aides understood the interests and attention span of the voters. They also understood that the press would have to cover Reagan as president; he could set the agenda—even if filled with staged events—and the news media would report it. The attitude of Reagan can be summed up this way: "Do what you want to do regardless of press criticism, don't rely exclusively on the press as intermediaries, and talk directly to the people."

With a forceful personality, a solid campaign strategy, and good advertising, a candidate can do this. In such instances, the news media once again become reporters, and their role as kingmakers is diminished.

In campaigning, the tug-of-war continues. In coverage of non-campaign political matters, such as the daily operation of government, press dominance meets less resistance.

Just as campaign coverage influences the amount of attention voters pay to candidates, so does news coverage of the day's events shape their perceptions of the world. Priorities about issues, especially remote or complex matters, are assigned based in large part on the importance ascribed to these issues by the news media.

The classic definition of this process continues to be, "The news media don't tell people what to think, but they tell people what to think about." Because of this influential role, the criteria used to define "news" should be carefully established. Whatever the press decrees to be significant, by putting it on page one or at the top of a newscast, automatically becomes important to a vast public.

That is simply a fact of life in this "information age," and the news media should not back off from their responsibility to make difficult choices about which stories deserve coverage. A related responsibility, however, is that of setting standards for that coverage.

Particularly with television, the medium tends to dictate the nature of the message. Time constraints and the incessant demand for "good pictures" affect scope and depth of coverage.

Television can deliver news clearly and forcefully, but it can also lapse into trivializing important stories. Sometimes this happens by design, as when a politician entices reporters into covering a pointless event. On many occasions, however, the news media (again, especially television) cause their own problems by reporting only the most superficial aspects of a story.

Reasoning for this apparently includes a fear that the public is uninterested in or incapable of understanding the background of issues. Unemployment can be graphically depicted in a story about an out-of-work man who has been reduced to begging to feed his children. That story performs some important functions: it alerts the public to the seriousness of a problem and it might spur some corrective action.

But *why* is this man out of work? Unemployment doesn't just happen. It is the result of a complicated chain of economic policies that probably stretches back many years. The history of the problem is hard to illustrate and explain, but it is nonetheless important to understanding the central issue.

News reporting and news consumption set standards for each other. If the news delivered to the public is superficial, people don't expect much else. If the audience doesn't expect more, news organizations do not feel compelled to deliver more. That cycle continues, wearing down the news product until it becomes intellectual mush.

No malevolence is behind this process; no conspiracy exists to deprive Americans of information. The problem is one of discipline: standards for news must be self-imposed, and that requires an institutional introspection that the news business rarely undertakes.

Ratings and circulation figures are good gauges of the success of the news industry as a business, but they do not measure the accomplishments of news organizations as educators or as integral parts of the complex socio-political organism that is American society today. Using only quantitative measures of press achievement is deceptive because doing so neglects the more qualitative judgments the news media must make about their performance.

In the rush of delivering the day's news, reporters, editors, and producers rarely have time to think about the effect their words and pictures will have and about how relied upon their products are. News does not exist in a vacuum. Most stories create ripples that spread in concentric rings, affecting many people and events and sometimes generating additional stories. All this leads back to the issue of press power: how is it wielded, how is it measured, and how is it controlled? These questions deserve more attention from the public and from the press itself.

When the products of non-news communications media are added to the flow of information Americans receive, the collective weight becomes immense. In politics, advertising may seem to support some news stories and contradict others. Sometimes the ads may strike voters as being more believable (or at least more appealing) than newscasts. Whatever relative weights are given to political news and ads, the sheer volume of this material threatens to overwhelm voters.

Few political ads are blatantly deceptive. The truth can usually be found somewhere, shaded though it might be. With its carefully planned appeal to emotion, this advertising can have profound effect on voting behavior.

Political ads might not be too different technically from the ads that sell soap, but buying soap and "buying" a president are two different matters. The electoral decisions political advertising helps bring about have lasting impact. The public can't switch to another president as easily as it can change brands of soap.

Campaign advertising deserves more oversight from press and public. As with political news coverage, such a concentration of power requires self-regulation and constant public scrutiny.

As Americans emerged from the 1986 campaigns and braced themselves for the presidential race and other elections of 1988, politicians and journalists seemed headed for their usual rough-and-tumble relationship. Skepticism about politicians' motives remains common; that is probably healthy and the pols know they can do little about it anyway. Despite lingering public uneasiness about the extent of press power, no substantive response to those concerns is likely.

The love-hate relationship between the public and the press is enduring. Millions of Americans will watch their favorite anchormen every night, absorbing some pieces of the information and entertainment the newscasts provide. As they partake of this feast of news, however, the public will not surrender its capacity for disbelief.

When seeing a story about a highly emotional issue, such as abortion, some of the news audience will believe the reporter has injected his or her own beliefs into the story. Persons agreeing with the reporter's purported viewpoint might not be bothered, but others will seize upon this as being yet another example of press bias.

To a considerable extent, journalists must shrug off this criticism. People sometimes see bias where none exists; any story that contradicts their own view becomes suspect. If news organizations were to refrain from publishing anything that might be controversial, the news would be short and dull every day.

On the other hand, the legitimate power of the press depends on public faith. For instance, when reporters uncover government corruption, the public must be predisposed to believe the press and must give the news accounts fair hearing. Otherwise, the press will be transformed from watchdog to lapdog. News professionals cannot be oblivious to what the public thinks about how they do their jobs.

No foolproof formula exists that can ensure resolute public trust in the news media. Public opinions about virtually everything fluctuate, and news professionals simply have to keep those fluctuations from becoming so extreme that press credibility suffers lasting damage. The news media must recognize they are not universally loved or even respected. Being loved isn't essential, but being respected is, and the press should exercise more diligence in earning that respect.

The public is more sensitive to press ethics than many journalists care to admit. Among the standards the public expects the press to follow are these:

• Even-handed treatment of competing candidates and ideas;

• Respect for an individual's privacy (even politicians deserve some respite from the searchlight of publicity);

• Resistance to making stories more sensational than they need be;

• Limited use of anonymous sources; avoidance of misrepresentation in gathering news;

• Correction of errors when they occur;

• Reasonable expertise by reporters in matters they cover;

• At least occasional display of compassion in the pursuit of news.

This litany of ethical issues is familiar as a theoretical basis for journalism, but in practice many of these standards are often ignored. Particularly in the tense atmosphere of a campaign, professional conduct can suffer. The public doesn't always notice these failings, but they do so often enough to increase skepticism about the good faith of journalists.

All this should not be dismissed as the stuff of esoteric debate. Anyone who watches, listens to, or reads the news, and votes, has a personal stake in the work done by communications professionals and politicians. This vested interest can be protected only if the individual understands the rules of the game and pays attention to how it is being played.

Just as politics is too important to be entrusted wholly to politicians, so too is the dissemination of information too important to be taken for granted. The news business, no less than politics, needs watchdogs.

News media power must be equaled by news media responsibility. This is a difficult but attainable goal. If it is achieved, the delicate balance between political power and media power can be maintained.

Bibliography

Arlen, Michael J. *Living-Room War.* Viking, 1969.

Broder, David S. *Behind the Front Page.* Simon & Schuster, 1987.

Cannon, Lou. *Reagan.* Putnam, 1982.

Cater, Douglass. *The Fourth Branch of Government.* Vintage, 1959.

Crouse, Timothy. *The Boys on the Bus.* Random House, 1973.

Deakin, James. *Straight Stuff.* Morrow, 1984.

Diamond, Edwin and Bates, Stephen. *The Spot.* MIT Press, 1984.

Germond, Jack W. and Witcover, Jules. *Blue Smoke and Mirrors.* Viking, 1981.

Henry, William A. *Visions of America.* Atlantic Monthly Press, 1985.

Jamieson, Kathleen Hall. *Packaging the Presidency.* Oxford, 1984.

Kelley, Stanley. *Professional Public Relations and Political Power.* Johns Hopkins, 1956.

Klein, Herbert G. *Making It Perfectly Clear.* Doubleday, 1980.

Mailer, Norman. *St. George and the Godfather.* Signet, 1972.

May, Ernest R. and Fraser, Janet (eds.). *Campaign '72: The Managers Speak.* Harvard, 1973.

McGinniss, Joe. *The Selling of the President 1968.* Trident Press, 1969.

Moore, Jonathan and Fraser, Janet (eds.). *Campaign for President: The Managers Look at '76.* Ballinger, 1977.

Powell, Jody. *The Other Side of the Story.* Morrow, 1984.

Ranney, Austin. *Channels of Power.* Basic Books, 1983.

Schram, Martin. *The Great American Video Game.* Morrow, 1987.

Shields, Mark. *On the Campaign Trail.* Algonquin, 1985.

Stoler, Peter. *The War Against the Press.* Dodd, Mead, 1986.

White, Theodore H. *America in Search of Itself.* Harper & Row, 1982.

White, Theodore H. *The Making of the President 1960.* Atheneum, 1961.

Witcover, Jules. *Marathon.* Viking Penguin, 1977.

Index

173